BEYOND ANGER:
On Being a Feminist in the Church

BEYOND ANGER:
On Being a Feminist in the Church

Carolyn Osiek, R.S.C.J.

PAULIST PRESS
New York/Mahwah

Library of Congress
Catalog Card Number: 85-62936

ISBN: 0-8091-2777-6

Published by Paulist Press
997 Macarthur Boulevard
Mahwah, New Jersey 07430

Printed and bound in the
United States of America

Contents

Preface

This book was written during part of my sabbatical year 1984–85 from Catholic Theological Union. I am grateful to the administration and faculty of CTU for their quality as colleagues and their generous encouragement, as well as to my religious community for their patient endurance of frequent progress reports. I also wish to thank the following for their enthusiastic response to parts of the book's contents and above all, their helpful suggestions: the faculty and the women students of CTU, 1983–84; the New Testament Group of the Chicago Cluster of Theological Schools; participants in the Professional Leadership Conference at the Lutheran School of Theology, Chicago, in May, 1984; Penny Gill; Rosemary Bearss, R.S.C.J.; the faculty and ministers who comprise the Hyde Park Women's Reading Group; the Trappistine community of Redwoods Monastery, Whitethorn, California; and the Religious of the Sacred Heart of the San Francisco and Menlo Park/San Jose areas.

To all the women in the above list, and to all the women of the Church who remain faithful members in spite of continual setbacks, this book is respectfully and gratefully dedicated.

Introduction

This is a book I had to write. There were other far easier and more enjoyable things I could have done with my sabbatical time. But I had to write it, for two reasons: I believe it needs to be said, and I need to say it. The book is neither an historical study, nor a case documentation, nor a personal account, though by the very nature of the topic personal experience will play an integral part.

The situation of women in the Catholic Church of the industrial and post-industrial countries today is moving rapidly toward crisis. In surprisingly increasing numbers, loyal, believing, church-going women are becoming aware of what the Church, to which they have in varying ways given much of their lives, has done with that gift. Homemakers have found that they are valued only for what they can cook or how well they can clean. Younger mothers have been told in many subtle ways, if not directly, that their responsibility takes priority over the development of any other kind of self-actualization or leadership. Older mothers who never raised such questions themselves are finding that their young adult daughters want to have nothing to do with an institution that, in the name of God, treats them like second-class citizens. Divorced and remarried women must choose between Church and marital happiness. Lesbian women are told it is all right to be who they are as long as they do not express their identity in relationship. The spiritual needs of working women are largely ignored by the official Church. Professional women are feared by many male Church authorities because they know enough not to passively submit to poor pastoral care. Vowed women religious who over the past twenty years have taken seriously the Church's mandate to spiritual and structural renewal in the wake of Vatican II find themselves mistrusted for the directions they have chosen by the very institution that gave them the mandate. Women who volunteer their services in some kind of pastoral ministry are often made to feel that they are only tolerated because of the shortage of priests. Women active in the ecumenical movement find insensitivity to their legitimate concerns in the name of "ecumenical sensitivity."

Women employed as pastoral ministers in hospitals, parishes, and student centers are usually hired by the priest in charge and can be fired by him or his successor with no recourse to a higher authority in the system which placed him there. After receiving good theological and pastoral training, they frequently find themselves in deteriorating pastoral situations with no power to effect change because those responsible are part of the problem. They have gifts for ministry and collaboration that go unappreciated because their employers are unused to their style and too threatened to consider change. The result is frustration, discouragement, burnout, and bitterness, often ending in complete alienation from the institutional Church.

What is striking about most of these women is that in spite of their frustrating, painful experience, they wish to remain loyal to the Church in which they have found both life and death. What is remarkable is that most of them somehow do. That is both "good news" and "bad news."

The bad news includes the personal toll such loyalty takes on persons full of energy, creativity, and idealism, much of which is simply annihilated in the process. It also includes the political reality that their labor and their lives are helping to shore up a structure which would be forced to face its need for reform much more quickly if they simply abandoned it. By staying, they are leaving themselves open to continued exploitation. For both these reasons, some have realized that the only way to preserve their personal integrity is to leave. Unfortunately, then, their prophetic voice is only heard on the way out the door, and never again.

The good news is that the majority who stay are giving expression to something deep within them, something closely bound up with their sense of their own identity. They are *loyal persons,* faithful in their relationships, loyal to persons to whom they have committed themselves, loyal to their God, and therefore loyal to the institution that has incarnated both human relationships and God for them. This means that the Church on its torturously slow way to renewal will continue to have them present with their gifts and sensitivity. Their prophetic voice can be raised and perhaps even heard with regularity. The price of this loyalty is for them a way of the cross.

It is to such as these that this book is directed: to those women who, although they know exactly what is happening, nevertheless decide to remain. The task for them is threefold: how to reconcile loyalty with experience which tells them such loyalty is foolish; how to cope with the situation while working for change; how to find hope.

I address myself primarily to women of the majority culture in the Roman Catholic Church in North America, because it is their situation that I know best. To the extent that what is said here is not applicable in other cultures and subcultures, let the reader take what she can, and re-express it in the language appropriate to other situations.

Much of what is said here is also applicable in other denominations. In those which ordain women, the dynamics are slightly different inasmuch as there is at least some official visibility of women in leadership. However, the patterns of prejudice and resentment, of fear and intimidation, of frustration and discouragement are surprisingly similar. Again, let the reader adapt or recreate what is written in these pages, but I suspect that for readers in most religious institutions of similar culture, there will be very little that needs adaptation.

The first chapter charts some of the stages of consciousness raising and explores what is likely to be the inner experience of the woman who is awakening in one way or another to the awareness of the patriarchal character of the Church and what that structure has meant to women.

The second chapter examines some of the ways which such a woman may adopt in order to adjust to her changed awareness and continue to function within her environment.

The third chapter suggests that there is only one way in the situation of impasse which results to choose life and continue to choose it without being unfaithful to deeply held convictions.

The fourth chapter attempts the frightening task of developing a theology of the cross for feminists as a response to the traditional belief in the possibility of redemptive suffering.

Finally, the conclusion offers some practical points for living in the everyday world the spirituality that has been traced throughout the book.

I spoke at the beginning of an approaching crisis. A crisis is not necessarily a bad thing. The original meaning of the word has to do with a moment of decision, hence a turning point toward a new direction. It also then came to mean a time of judgment, when truth and falsehood, right and wrong would be made manifest, and when the cause of accused persons would be vindicated, or their guilt proven. I believe the coming crisis for women in the churches contains elements of both meanings.

Certainly we are moving toward some kind of turning point, which may be formed by conscious choices and changed policies, or by loss of the most creative people, declining attendance, and subsequent loss of vitality in the churches. For other reasons, this has already happened to Catholicism in many European countries. It has the potential of happening in North America as well. Women in many Protestant denominations know well that a vote to ordain women does not solve all problems; in fact, it creates as many as it solves. Spiritual vitality necessitates good policies, but it has more to do with conversion.

We are also, I believe, somehow under judgment. Declining numbers of candidates for religious orders and priesthood cannot be attributed primarily to human mistakes, but must first of all be referred to God who, according to any theology of ministry, gives the original call. This decline is in fact dragging the Church, sometimes kicking and screaming, toward new forms of ministry, new roles for its less honored members, and new ways of living out its mission to preach the Gospel. We all stand accused, some of prejudice and hard-heartedness, some of willful blindness, others of lack of courage and allowing pain to turn to bitterness because that is easier. We all have to answer for our conduct, not only at the last judgment, but also at the current one.

Chapter One

THE PROCESS OF AWARENESS

In the spring of 1977, I was asked as one of the Research-Resource Associates in Women's Studies at Harvard Divinity School to give one of the presentations in the Theological Opportunities Program, a series of continuing education lectures for women in the area.

The choice of topic was mine. I had been doing research on women in the biblical world, so I was quite familiar with the scholarship and thinking up to that point about the difficult biblical texts which deal with women. More important, I had been experiencing some of the more strained aspects of the process of awakening which I shall describe below. I decided to put those two elements together, and give a talk that was at once scholarly and personal, that spoke of how I as feminist, biblical scholar, and believer was struggling with the conflict produced by that combination.[1] The response was overwhelming. Women from a variety of backgrounds and denominations, none of them professional theologians, could identify with what I was saying and push the questions further. After charting my own experience on the journey thus far, I ended the lecture with the words: "Now I'm waiting to find out what the next step is."

That was seven years ago. Since then, there have of course been a number of "next steps." I have seen them in myself and in other women as well. Though we each experience according to our own mode and capacity, there are some general patterns to the journey as it is undertaken by every woman who comes to some kind of feminist awareness. Those patterns are common to

7

any kind of movement from fear, darkness, and enslavement to courage, light, and liberation: the struggle to be freed from economic, racial, or attitudinal oppression by others; the struggle to be freed of one's self-inflicted chains through psychotherapy. What is traced here are the stages on the journey toward claiming one's own identity as Christian woman in the face of a tradition and community that have not generally been receptive to that journey.

Rejection and Fear

Today it is almost impossible for anyone in a Western country who is in contact with the communications media not to know the word "feminism" and to have at least some vague connotations associated with it, accurate or not. But it is another thing to have a concept, a reality, a movement directly confront me in my own daily experience, as something with which I have to come to terms.

Feminism today bears the burden of multivalent descriptions and definitions. There is no one right answer to the question, What is it? This is true for several reasons. One is that it is a movement which encompasses not just one aspect of modern life (economics, social class, religion, etc.) but the whole of it, not just the private or public sector, but both, not just personal or communal identity, but both. Unlike classism or racism, sexism is embedded at the core of human relationship, and is therefore inescapable.

Another reason for the ambiguity surrounding feminism is that women are not an isolable group in society, but permeate all of it. Our experiences, our aspirations, and our strategies are as different as our variety of backgrounds. Still another reason for possible confusion about feminism is that it is a movement which has by now been around long enough in its contemporary manifestation to have diversified, splintered, and taken off in many quite different directions. Many who would call themselves feminists can neither agree with nor approve of the directions taken by other feminists. Many others think that their sisters who have chosen a more moderate way have sold out to the male establishment, be it political, economic, or religious. The confusion and disagreement in the ranks do not foster clarity, but they are signs of life and growth.

Feminism in nearly every society in the world is at some point along the way to causing social upheaval. In some cultures, the revolutionary aspects are not yet visible; in some cultures, they have just begun. In the United States, they are increasingly unavoidable. "Upheaval" is not too strong a word. The effects on marriage, family, sexual identity, and many other patterns of relationship have not yet been adequately documented.

So, too, in the churches. Theology, ministry, church order, worship, and devotional life are being affected in some obvious ways (e.g. discussion of ordination of women; changes to inclusive language) and some not so obvious ways (e.g. increasing attention to the topic of women in papal statements; use of one's position on women's ordination as a test case for clerical and episcopal orthodoxy).

It is hardly surprising that the first reaction of a woman confronted with this reality is fear. The vast majority of women now in adulthood, regardless of social class, have been and are still being taught by family, the educational system, and the media that their most effective way of expressing themselves in the world is through a man, that they will never do anything outside the home as well as he does, and that to even try to do so is to risk rejection. Even women who are forced by their economic situation to work and have done so successfully for years can carry within themselves this set of assumptions. Veteran career women often bear a burden of self doubt far heavier than that of their male colleagues. For women in the churches, even in professional church ministry, the attitude takes the form of the unconscious assumption that anyone in a clerical collar can do it better. How many women parishioners still bypass the lay minister of Communion in favor of a priest? The subtle programming is long-term and deeply embedded.

The effect on a woman's self-perception can be devastating. However, there is also a comforting, secure aspect to all of this, as long as she is not pushed to perform in new and unfamiliar roles. The married woman who becomes fearful of driving because she is convinced that her husband does it better, the working woman who does not dare ask for a raise for fear of losing her job, the professional woman who fears to protest sexual discrimination or harassment because of possible job backlash, the woman minister who allows herself to be convinced that her way of ministering will not work, all have fallen into acquiescence to the myth of male superiority. Being able to abdicate ultimate responsibility, even at the price of repression, has a certain comfort.

Many such women simply do not realize what they have done to themselves all their lives, and thus can answer honestly, as far as conscious awareness informs them, that indeed they are not oppressed, are very happy with their lives, and have no need of being "liberated." For those on the other hand who have suffered enough to know what is happening to them, questioning again the presuppositions for their accommodating behavior, reopening areas of doubt, fear, and potential suffering, can be quite terrifying. It is far easier to leave well enough alone.

Turning Point Experiences

Eventually, however, it is no longer possible to leave well enough alone. Some are drawn through curiosity to see what this "women's liberation thing" is all about, and find that, quite unexpectedly, something of it speaks to their experience and even gives them a new perspective on that experience. Some have personal contacts, friends who have thought through the issues, and who give them feminist literature, invite them to a feminist meeting, or simply have a heart-to-heart talk about what is happening in their lives. Some find that "those feminists," whom they had always thought of as radical, strident (How many *men* have you heard called "strident" lately?), and very different from themselves are not as different as they had imagined. Others out of desire to be well-informed about current social trends read feminist literature and find it is not as off-the-mark as they had expected. Still others come unaided by anything or anyone to the point of sheer frustration and realization that their lives cannot continue as they have been.

A change in consciousness then brings on a changed interpretation of events. One's reaction to certain key points, triggering experiences, makes it no longer possible to deny that a personal upheaval has begun. For a married woman, the one millionth put-down remark by her husband makes her suddenly aware that he does not take her seriously as a person, and that she has allowed and even encouraged his attitude for years by her silent acceptance and thus tacit agreement. A woman office worker suddenly finds her employer's patronizing remarks one too many. A woman workshop leader discovers that her adult audience checks out the content of her lectures with her male teammate behind her back. A woman physician finds behind her male colleagues' remarks about their female patients the unspoken and unexamined diagnosis of hypochondria, which she never noticed before and which she now finds insulting. The woman pastoral worker hears for the first time the unarticulated doubt of priests and parishioners (male and female) that what she says is really correct teaching of the Church. The woman who has labored and hoped for greater rapport among churches finally realizes that *her* church is willing to sacrifice the rights of its women to achieve it. The faithful churchgoing woman begins to really notice for the first time that only men stand at the altar, that even if women enter the sanctuary, only males wear the distinctive clothing that sets them off as officially belonging there, that the language of worship does not seem to include her, that only men make authoritative religious pronouncements, and that when the media want the *official* opinion on religious matters, only men in clerical suits are consulted. Moreover, when she raises questions about these things, she is looked upon as radical. The woman theology student in a seminary asks a perceptive question in class and realizes from the student reaction that she is resented by some of her fellow students as a usurper rather than a potential companion in the work of proclaiming the Gospel.

Nearly every woman who comes to a feminist awareness can recount certain definite experiences like those described above. They may have been situations that were repeated many times before, but suddenly the old story becomes an event that takes on new meaning. Or there may be a one-time experience that comes at just the right moment to serve as live illustration of a new awareness of a disordered social world. Such an event is a true turning point because it evokes a crisis. Life is not as it was before, and can never be so again. It cannot return to the comfort of denial. One's self-image of loyalty and one's experience of oppression come to a screeching collision with one another and seem henceforth incompatible. How can I remain loyal to a person, institution, or tradition that has done this to me? But without that commitment, what do I have left? Who am I? This intense experience of dissonance provokes a predictable reaction.

Anger

If there is any one negative image that is most frequently attached to feminism by those who fear it, it is that of "those angry women." Anger in women seems to jar loose a great deal of primitive and irrational terror from both men and women who observe it. For Freudians, it evokes fear of rejection and separation from the Mother. Jungians see it as the embodiment of the violent and vindictive Anima. The receptive, nurturing aspect of the feminine, so desperately needed in a violent world, seems to have been abandoned to the destructive forces of human darkness. When women do not stabilize society, society is not stabilized.

Anger is a useful emotion. It mobilizes for defense, it makes it possible to engage and overcome a threatening enemy. It can also alienate those who do not perceive themselves as the enemy. It is nevertheless the natural and appropriate response of those women who find themselves in the situation of awakening described above. Coming into immediate awareness of how I have been diminished as a person, whether directly and intentionally by those immediately available to me, or indirectly through social structures and the cumulative effects of history, can provoke little else.

Anger is not a socially respectable feeling to express in our culture. The angry person is thought to be lacking in self-control and to be too weak to employ an appropriate assertiveness. This is already true in male culture; how much more so in female culture—in men's expectations of women and women's expectations of themselves. Thus the woman who begins to feel this appropriate anger may choose not to appropriately express it. As with any repressed anger, the result is depression and sadness: loss of energy, of zest, of a taste for life, inability to pray or to relate in a trusting and loving way with anyone. This feeling of isolation can lead to severe self-doubt and self-hatred, as if she herself were to blame for the predicament. "If I hadn't read that book"; "if I hadn't listened to that person"; "if I hadn't let it all get to me, I'd still be able to function normally." The price of repression is personal diminishment.

The woman who on the other hand chooses to express that

anger risks misunderstanding and rejection. There is no other phase of consciousness-raising that is as difficult to deal with, as threatening to others, as liable to elicit impatience and intolerance. The angry feminist is indiscriminately stereotyped and shunned by nearly everyone who is not in the same predicament. Most men find her sharp, critical, apt to condemn them for unknown offenses. Even the husband, pastor, or male colleague who prides himself on patience and understanding finds that his patience wears thin when he is treated as if he, too, is one of the oppressors, since he has taken great pains to prove himself to be on her side. Women in the first phase of rejection and fear described above find her extremely threatening, for she embodies everything they do not want to be. Women in the second phase of grappling with events that are provoking crises for them do not want to be confronted with what they might become. Women who have passed beyond the angry stage find it embarrassing and awkward to associate with someone who demonstrates a past mode of their own behavior which they would prefer to forget because it recalls too much pain.

Thus the angry woman is forced to find her support predominantly among other angry women. This is both helpful and detrimental. It is helpful because the exchange of stories and venting of feelings falls on sympathetic ears. She knows the comforting feeling of being heard and understood by others who are enduring the same fate. Support groups and rap sessions can be a kind of group therapy. They perform the very valuable function of allowing a woman the space and freedom to work through anger in a supportive environment so that the feelings do not fester and become destructive to her and to others.

There is, however, also a detrimental aspect to the mutual support of persons angry about the same issues. They can sometimes be so supportive of one another that the anger is reinforced and entrenched instead of being processed with a view to change and transformation. When this happens a kind of stagnation sets in, and the full *expression* of anger rather than its repression can lead to depression, sadness, personal and collective self-pity, and a sense of hopelessness. A woman who realizes this is happening to her must change her environment if she is ever to be free from the destructiveness of her own anger.

This experience of anger can last for years, requiring an enormous amount of patience on the part of others and of the woman herself. I do not believe it can ever be completely set aside. Unlike most other groups struggling for liberation, there is for many women no natural support group of persons surrounding them who are experiencing the same thing at the same time. That is why it is important and even necessary for them to seek out the kind of supportive presence that they need at the time. Learning socially acceptable modes of personal assertiveness helps them in the meantime to find a middle ground between the self-deprecation of the past and the overbearing aggressiveness of the felt present, so that they need not alienate well-meaning colleagues, family, and associates in the process.

The feeling and expression of anger is the necessary and appropriate response which rises up from the depths of one's being. It is a revolt against the personal and collective memory of accumulated pain: the pain of being treated as a child, an incompetent, a non-person in a society and faith community that verbally acclaim the equality and dignity of all. It cannot be bypassed without grave harm. Once entered into, it is never totally left behind. Forgiveness is not forgetfulness. It does not take away the issues.

Yet the healthy person cannot and should not remain angry forever. Anger is no final resting place. Eventually one becomes weary of it and longs for another way of being. Before another way can be embraced, however, anger must give way to something even less pleasant.

Broken Symbol Systems

As has already been emphasized, anger is a completely appropriate response to the awareness of oppression. It is also, however, an effective cover for other emotions. There is still some dignity, some appearance of control when one can lash out at the enemy and thus defend oneself. What anger can effectively hide is the pain and sadness that emerge whenever they are allowed to surface. To be, and even worse to *admit* to being, hurt and depressed leaves one quite vulnerable, which is exactly what the struggling feminist does not want to be. The old stereotypes of women as emotional, easily hurt, needing to be protected and taken care of, lurk in the background like ghosts of a past that has been abandoned and rejected because it was too easily exploited. To keep the ghosts in the cellar requires a great deal of effort, and once they get out, they wreak havoc on a tightly-controlled upper story.

They cannot be locked up forever. A semblance of control can be maintained as long as there is a salvageable sense of meaning, as long as the social and psychic constructions of reality remain credible. What eventually unleashes the dark side is the loss of those constructions through the disintegration of symbol systems. Psychologists and sociologists of knowledge point out to us how we build for ourselves a world of meaning through the mediation of symbols and relationships. Unconsciously we weave around ourselves a complex system in which we incorporate all important data into some kind of integrated whole. Bits of information that cannot be absorbed into the system are rejected, or, if too significant to be rejected, provoke a crisis which can be resolved only by the readjustment of the whole system to accommodate them.

What happens when important elements of that symbol system collapse? A profound sense of crisis results. This is what has happened to the many women who have found that because of their new awareness, they can no longer go on living as they had before. The reasons they had previously given for being and doing as they were accustomed no longer hold. To deliberately remain in an oppressive situation seems unhealthy and even destructive. They had formerly interpreted their pattern of relationships in marriage, employment, and church in such a way as to feel fully participative, but now they realize that in some very significant ways they have been excluded, patronized, exploited.

For the woman of faith, this awareness can bring about a religious crisis of severe proportions. She comes to feel as if the whole of her faith tradition has betrayed her by what it has done to women throughout its history. She sees the institutional Church and all its male leaders as participants in, if not perpetrators of, a concerted effort to undermine the human dignity, subdue the initiative, and control the lives of its women. There is no need to exaggerate or invent evidence; for those who have eyes to see, there is ample evidence from the New Testament to the present papacy that this has indeed happened. It is unnecessary to document here the research that has been done by feminists in recent years on the effects of misogynist attitudes and policies on women in the Church.[2]

Nor is it helpful to appeal to the positive side of the history, to point out all the good things that have been said and done by and for women. This approach is somewhat like telling the person who has been assaulted and injured that she or he is lucky not to have been killed. It does nothing whatsoever to ease the trauma of what has happened. Besides, behind every positive point that can be made lurks the shadow of discrimination. If Catherine of Siena and Teresa of Avila were declared Doctors of the Church, they were also severely harassed and hampered by the ecclesiastical establishment of their day. If Mary has been exalted in the tradition above all other creatures, there has still been an adamant rejection of the aspect of the feminine in God, and an unquestioned acceptance of the masculine as symbol of divine personhood.

The credibility of the institutional Church as sacrament,

bearer of salvation, and something worth a lifetime of commitment is at stake. Many good women have simply made the judgment that it is no longer worth the pain and struggle to stay with
it. The Church is thus immensely impoverished by the loss of
talent, creativity, and leadership potential. Most women who
choose this way do not do so lightly. They recognize it as the only
way to survive psychically and spiritually. Some go to another
denomination where they think they can find more breathing
space, only to discover often that while public policies and official practices differ, attitudes and unspoken politics may not be
so different after all. Others band together in new faith communities where they can be spiritually nourished, but at the price
of being cut off from a tradition that they have loved. Most
choose to stay and try to work out a mode of survival that is at
least as life-giving as it is destructive.

The sense of loss goes far deeper than that of church membership, however. It extends to the core of one's belief system.
The vastly perpetrated myth of the maleness of God has established maleness as the norm of humanity created in "his" image.
This is "myth" in the true sense: not a fabricated idea, but a powerful story that once set in motion continues through its own set
of symbols to shape meaning and identity for those who claim
the story as their own.

The astute observer of Judeo-Christian history is aware of
how the persistent attempts to image God as feminine have been
carefully and almost embarrassedly tucked away as quirks at best
and aberrations at worst. In spite of the conclusions of most theologians to the contrary, the collective social and psychological
effect has been to render the feminine non-normative for imaging God. The reactions ranging from uncomfortable laughter to
outright offense when feminine language and imagery are used
for God are indicative of how unimaginable such a thing still is
to most people, simply because they have been deprived of that
aspect of the theological tradition.

The affront to one's being that this one-sidedness represents can only be appreciated by someone whose social identity
is excluded from the divine imaging: an exclusively white God
with middle-class values is just as offensive for those whose identity is otherwise. The religious experience of one who has grown
accustomed to the assumption that God is "like me" is quite different from the experience of the one who knows that God is
"like the other," a being with whom I cannot identify according
to the analogy of my specific personhood.

For the Christian woman there is the added complication
of the maleness of Christ, which is proclaimed down the centuries from icons, mosaics, crucifixes, and statues. It is there over
our altars, on our walls, and in our books. It is incarnated in the
male priest who claims to represent Christ presiding over his
community. The male Christ strides through history with the
face of a Byzantine Pantocrator: serene, powerful, triumphant.
In his name women have been silenced and demeaned, told not
only that they cannot image God but that they cannot even image
God's most human manifestation. The maleness of Christ, not-
withstanding all the contemporary theological anthropology that
has tried to correct it, has stood and still stands as a barrier between women and God. The mediator has become the obstacle.
If a woman cannot find an "I" mirrored either in God or in
Christ, what is left?

For the Catholic, there is Mary, the woman exalted above
all other merely human beings. But Mary has always been carefully distinguished from God. Any attempts at worship or even
what could be construed to go beyond the bounds of strictly con-
trolled honoring have been suppressed whenever possible. That
they continue to exist anyway in many popular religious cultures
reveals the unconscious human need for a feminine dimension
in what is worshiped, in spite of the rational denials of such a
need on the part of the institution.

Even as an honored creature, however, the Mary of tradition contains mixed signals, as feminists are quite aware. On one hand she is the most exalted of God's creation, motivating the exaltation of womanhood along with her to the "pedestal." On the other hand, she is thus held up as an impossible ideal to which no woman could attain, in comparison with whom all women are invited to feel inadequate. Moreover, in spite of the excellent theological attempts to distinguish the "historical Mary" from the "Mary of faith" and to portray her as glorified because of her superior faith and discipleship,[3] the impression remains that her chief qualification for exaltation is maternity. Even for Mary, biology is destiny.

An important component of one's religious universe is ritual, the gestures, symbols, and words which are familiarly repeated at significant moments to reinforce faith and community identity. For Catholics and many other Christians, the central and most significant ritual is the Eucharist. It is the enactment through which the Christian community most clearly declares its identity as the assembly of believers who look to what Jesus did in the past, who in that very remembrance affirm the hidden work of the reign of God in the present, and who by looking to the past proclaim his coming in the future.

The Eucharist is truly the center of Christian life. For the feminist believer it has become as well the center of paradox and even contradiction. She knows that it has been and is still being used as a means of control, withheld as punishment from those who would question authority, even withheld from those who have the right to it but are deprived because they live in areas with few priests while ordination regulations inhibit the raising up of priests from the community. What is signified socially in the celebration is that the celibate male is the norm of Christian personhood, for only he can image Christ to the community in this unique and special way. Moreover, ordination is in the present structure still the means of access to most positions of authority or responsibility that can make a difference. Thus the celebration of Eucharist is the ever present reminder that, no matter what the rhetoric, women and men simply are not equal in the Church. Any discussion of the exclusivity of ordination which pretends that equality is not part of the issue is either dishonest or naive.

All of this can make it exceedingly difficult for the feminist believer not only to derive any spiritual nourishment from the celebration of the central faith mystery but even sometimes to attend, knowing that presence implies participation. If it were only a matter of remaining absent from Eucharist out of protest, it would be simple enough. But the habits of many years cannot so easily be set aside, nor the support systems abandoned. The woman who allows herself the full awareness of what is happening realizes that her whole religious symbol system is disintegrating. It is one thing to say that human persons have misused the name of God, the person of Christ, and the mystery of the Eucharist to further their own interests and prevent full recognition of the humanity and full dignity of women. It is another thing to say that God has stood idly by and let it all happen. If this is so, we have an uncaring or an impotent God.

Thus the ability to pray, the very ability to trust and believe in God is at stake. Even if a woman can rationally convince herself that there is a God who does not will the exclusion and the suffering it causes, how then has it been allowed to happen? The usual answer is of course the sinfulness of members of the Church, the institution which is both holy and imperfect at the same time. For many women, however, this is not enough; their own sense of integrity leads them to search for entirely different images of God than those with which they have heretofore been familiar. This is practically a search in the dark, for the feminist tradition has barely begun to discover new images and symbols that have lasting transpersonal value.

So for many there is nothing to adequately replace what was once of supreme importance. The sense of loss and collapse of meaning which comes from this faith crisis can be acute, even paralyzing. What makes it even worse is that the faith crisis often provokes or is related to any number of similar crises in family, social relationships, and work, as though working through one dimension at a time were not sufficient.

Impasse

Once the feminist believer has allowed herself to experience the collapse of her religious symbol system, she will be led inevitably still further downward to the low point at which paralysis seems to harden and become the only way: to impasse. This is a total awareness "which insinuates itself inescapably and uninvited into one's inner life and growth and into one's relationships." Here there is a sense that no movement is possible, that "every normal manner of acting is brought to a standstill," and that "ironically, impasse is experienced not only in the problem itself but also in any solution rationally attempted."[4]

There seems to be no viable way out, no way that can be freely chosen and embraced. To continue living as before would necessitate more denial than most people are capable of. To remain angry and to vent that anger in a considerable amount of protest seems futile because there is no evidence that the situation will change substantially in the near future, nor that those capable of changing it understand or care in any great numbers; thus to remain perpetually angry seems self-destructive. To attempt to make traditional forms of prayer and worship meaningful when they are not would create unbearable tension and a sense of dishonesty. To take up a kind of marginal existence within the Church, neither fully in nor fully out, is a difficult and lonely path to pursue. To walk away from community and tradition would cause greater isolation, aloneness, perhaps guilt, and certainly rootlessness. No alternative feels acceptable, let alone desirable.

Depression, emptiness, and joylessness are symptomatic of the experience of impasse. There is a sense of having been abandoned: by friends, male and female, who said they understood; by those to whom one looked for leadership and inspiration; by God. All forms of support previously relied upon seem to have been pulled out. It is a death experience, a dark night, to which all the descriptions of such abandonment and desolation in the spiritual classics are applicable.[5] The forces of creation and destruction, of life and death, of consolation and desolation seem to come from the same source and to be at war within the person. It is a spiritual crisis of enormous proportions, and must be understood and treated as such.

The woman who finds herself in this situation is attempting to maintain "dual membership" in the world of church and that of feminism at the same time. She is attempting to wait it out and hope that somehow they will be compatible. But to her dismay she may find that she is regarded with suspicion by both groups because of their mistrust of each other. Most persons who represent the interests of institutional churches are less than welcoming to what they consider the "stridency" of the feminist movement. Likewise most convinced feminists who are not attracted to religious faith or church affiliation have little sympathy for anyone who is. What is even worse, the woman herself may not be able to fully trust representative members of either group because neither represents or even understands sufficiently her own position. Thus the sense of anomie, loss, and rootlessness is heightened. By trying to belong in two camps, she may not be fully accepted in either.[6] She is faced with the problem of preserving a sense of self without being affirmed by significant others, and of being *in* two worlds but not fully *of* either one.

Is there any way out of this predicament? A way must be found, but it can only be found by remaining in darkness, *with* the sense of impasse. As with all suffering, there is no resolution by dodging or attempting to deny the pain. The way out is the way through, beyond the impasse between rational and irrational modes of existence.

Breakthrough

One of the characteristics of a true impasse is that "the more action one applies to escape it, the worse it gets." The familiar acquired skills for problem solving do not work. Analysis, strategy, and logic are inadequate to deal with the situation. True and lasting change can be brought about only by skills and solutions that are of a wholly different order. New principles and foundations, a new vision of reality must be discovered, which will give new perspectives and suggest new directions for forward movement. This can happen only if the pain and the severe sense of limit that impasse entails are fully embraced and assimilated.[7]

In this transforming process, religious symbols and belief formulations will inevitably change. The old ways that were meaningful before the advent of darkness and impasse are dead and cannot be revived. But eventually they will be replaced by new images and symbols, so that what was once considered loss will begin to appear as gain. How this breakthrough process actually takes shape will be explored in the third chapter.

Chapter Two
WAYS OF COPING

Having seen the outline of the process by which a believing woman is likely to come to awareness of her situation as woman in a patriarchal Church, we turn now to the theme of "living with reality." Once such a woman knows the implications of her situation, she must choose first of all whether or not to remain in it. This is no easy decision. It is a question of assessing the cost and making a conscious evaluation whether, first of all, she can survive the toll it will take on her and remain in psychological and spiritual health.

The second assessment is whether or not it is worth the pain. The journey described in the first chapter can be drawn out for years and move more in circles than in a straight line. It is by no means clear that the direction of growth and challenge for everyone is to remain in an oppressive situation. Psychology would in fact say quite the contrary. For some, the choice of life and growth necessarily calls them outside the structures of the institutional churches to the growing communities of women who are searching for new religious symbols, new ways of worshiping together, and the beginnings of new faith traditions. For them the breakthrough moments will come as they experience the peace of knowing the way that is right for them, and in the discovery of new ways of being faith-filled women outside traditional structures.

Theirs is of necessity a rejectionist stance, for they feel they must turn their back on the whole of the religious tradition in order to remain whole persons. Their judgment is that the entire tradition is hopelessly corrupted by the sin of patriarchalism, and

thus unredeemable. This is a serious accusation, one with which
every representative of that same religious tradition must come
to grips. The sinful human face of the Church is here judged to
be such a determinative factor in what the Church has been and
even could become, that there is really no hope of conversion,
and therefore redemption, for it. As in the parallel cases of racism and classism, the Church stands under the judgment of the
oppressed who cry to God for redress.

In the case of the rejectionist, the cry has turned to indifference. The only way to cope with the pain is to remove its cause
as a significant factor in one's life. This involves the loss of some
important goods as well: a sense of belonging to an ongoing community with a tradition, and widespread community support.
She runs the risk of rootlessness, anomie, loss of a sense of belonging, and loneliness. Only the support of other women who
have made a similar choice can make a difference. Together they
must forge new bonds of loving community and create new traditions.[1]

This book, however, is about the others. What happens to
those who discern that their call is to remain within the traditional religious structures, regardless of the personal cost? How
does one learn to live with the psychological and spiritual pain
that this entails? There are a number of possible alternative ways
in which they will come to terms with their situation at various
points along the journey and develop coping behavior that is still
more or less acceptable and allows for survival—sometimes even
for change. These ways will be explored below.

The key question posed by the rejectionists must be dealt
with by every religious feminist, regardless of her stance: is the
oppression of patriarchy separable from the Judeo-Christian tradition? Racism and classism, as well as sexism, have been publicly disavowed by most mainstream churches, yet those same
churches seem extremely reluctant at times to undergo the
changes necessary to make practice consistent with policy. This

is especially true in the case of sexism. In spite of bold statements advocating the elimination in society of every form of discrimination based on sex, institutional church leaders seem for the most part oblivious of the ways in which the very structures and practices of liturgy and decision making reinforce the patriarchal image of power and thus contradict their stated policy. An optimistic view of human nature, religious institutions, and history could say all that is lacking is education and consciousness-raising; a more pessimistic view would question whether there is any hope of radical change, i.e., genuine conversion and renewal.

Are the tradition, the institution which conveys it, and the people who embody that tradition and perpetuate that institution capable of conversion from the sin of sexism? Is the tradition redeemable? This is the central issue. While the rejectionist answers no to that query, all of those described below answer yes. The question then becomes, How? Each woman gives a different answer.

Marginalist

Barbara is a divorcee with two children in their early teens. Once active in parish life, she had been a lector and member of the parish council. Her consciousness began to be raised when, though she had received grave warnings from her doctor of serious medical complications if she conceived another child, her pastor informed her that any medically-induced form of contraception would be seriously sinful, and her husband refused to cooperate with any natural method. Her anger grew and began to be expressed; divorce followed not long afterward. Even though she has not remarried, she dropped out of regular church attendance, then joined a feminist worship group which she attends regularly on Sunday mornings. Asked if she still considers herself a Catholic, she bristles. The question is too threatening to answer. She is worried about religious affiliation for her children, who no longer attend church, either. She sees the inconsistency which they point out between her position and her nagging at them to go to church, but cannot bring herself to do anything more than what she is doing.

Some women find themselves at the fringes of church life because of their level of consciousness and their stance. Lacking the clear call or the courage to leave, neither can they fully belong. Their loyalty hangs like an albatross around their necks because it deals only death and no life. The marginalist is often an angry person, one whose anger festers and goes only in destructive directions because her energies have no creative outlet.

The marginalist is apt to avoid all participation in public liturgy and to participate in small informal worship groups only if the style is one that is acceptable to her and the persons involved are well known. She has difficulty with most faith propositions and exists in a state of spiritual emptiness, not knowing what she believes or wants to believe, what she feels or wants to feel about religious matters. The hurt has gone so deep that the only possible response is numbness or its defense: anger. While unable to identify with anything distinctive of her faith tradition, she will nevertheless not let go of her proclaimed identification with the whole of it.

The most difficult aspect of this kind of existence is suggested by the name itself. Being on the margin means never being near the center of anything. The margin is a very good place to be for short periods of time, while adjusting to a new position and new consciousness. A place in the shadows allows for greater freedom to explore and to change than does a position in the limelight, where attention and expectations are constantly present. In every major life change there are temporary phases of transition between what was and what will be, a time when we can only say what we have been but are no longer. This state of limbo then eventually gives way to a new identity and a new place in the circle, or perhaps in another circle.

The woman here called "marginalist," by contrast, is one who cannot escape from existence on the edge into a new place. She is stuck there, and thus cannot really feel part of anything, significant in any process, or valued by anyone within the religious body. Her anger may be her only viable means of expression. Tragically, it alienates her even more from others. While the person who rejects the tradition and attempts to step completely out of it says no to the possibility of conversion on the part of the patriarchal institution, the marginalist seems to reject the possibility of conversion for herself as well.

Loyalist

Peggy is a warmly affectionate young woman from a strongly and conservatively religious family, recently married to a man of similar background. She is very active in several different kinds of church service organizations. Her close ties with her family are of immense importance to her. She is always reliable, supportive, respectful of authority, and liked by everyone. Though she had wanted to get a part-time job to help bring in some income before beginning a family, her husband did not want it, and she considered pleasing him more important. During an adult education series at her parish, some questions arose about the place of women in the Church. They became her questions, too. She was encouraged to pursue them by the young assistant pastor and the director of religious education, with whom she had several long and helpful conversations. Her parents and husband, however, strongly disapproved of her getting into issues that are "only pushed by troublemakers." The whole experience is very difficult for her because being less than agreeable and pleasing causes her deep conflict. She knows, however, that she cannot abandon the questions once they have been raised. Her solution is to plunge even more intensely into the kinds of religious activities in which she has been involved, in hopes of bringing about changes in the awareness and attitudes of the people with whom she works there. She sees it as her special apostolate to quietly and loyally raise questions which will make people think and eventually bring them around to changing the way men and women relate to each other in the Church.

At quite a different place on the spectrum from the marginalist is the "loyalist." While the marginalist cannot bring herself to give up her loyalty, it is nothing but a burden to her. For the loyalist, on the contrary, it is her link with tradition and thus her way of participation and preserving a sense of belonging. Whether through intellectual conviction or affective attachment or both, the loyalist holds as a starting point the essential goodness and holiness of the religious tradition as revelation and gift from God. That revelation as contained in Scripture and embodied in the tradition and in competent authority needs no external validation by contemporary human experience. It cannot by its very nature be oppressive or unjust, since it comes from God. The true content of revelation, properly understood, must speak for genuine freedom and humanization according to the divine plan.

The problem, then, is with the recipients of that revelation. It is the human vehicles who are imperfect, sinful, oppressive, unjust. It is they who falsify the Word by subjecting it to abusive interpretations which are not faithful to God's intent. The breakdown has occurred in the reception of the message, not in the message itself, nor even in the original conveyors or authoritative interpreters of the message. The writers of Scripture and the other persons responsible for the earliest formation of the tradition were somehow specially protected from the kinds of error and tunnel vision which later generations demonstrated. Thus the revelation of God as embodied in Scripture and tradition stands free of the corruptive influences of the history of fallen humanity.

Along with this theological position comes the correlate assumption that if we could only discover the true meaning of troublesome segments of revelation, especially of difficult Scripture passages, we would find that life according to the divine plan is not oppressive at all, that true happiness lies in following it, and that men and women are meant to live in mutual love and respect, which can only be achieved by heeding that divine plan.[2]

The loyalist position issues a call to conversion. It proclaims the need for true humanization which will mean transformation after the pattern of God's intention for humanity. To do this it can engage in careful exegesis of biblical and church texts that seem oppressive of women in order to demonstrate that they are not really oppressive at all, but have seemed so because they have been improperly interpreted. It can also at times accept the traditional argument that social order can come only through some kind of hierarchy (in this case, of men over women), that this is simply a God-given ordering which in no way implies superiority-inferiority, but that on the contrary this is the only way to find happiness in relationship as believers in God. The popular Country and Western song, "Stand By Your Man" expresses this position very well in non-religious and highly emotive language.

While long on patience and courage, the loyalist solution is short on rigorous intellectual analysis. Even if it *may* have been true in some cultures of the ancient Mediterranean world, or for that matter in some cultures today, that the hierarchical ordering of male over female did not imply gender superiority in the minds of those who lived with it, any analysis of social patterns in contemporary Western cultures indicates otherwise. By insisting that the patterns of relationships as laid out in Scripture, once properly understood, are normative for subsequent generations, the loyalist is forced to deny that history is revelatory, i.e., that God continues to be present in events and new insights. The ways of thinking and relating that were the context for the biblical writers and the formation of the classical religious tradition become, even in spite of conscious intention to the contrary, crystallized as superior to any others. If we find them wanting, the problem is ours: we have not adequately understood them. Along with the asset of the call to conversion comes the liability of the too-easy imposition of guilt.

The other way in which the loyalist is hindered from exercising rigorous intellectual honesty is in the temptation to stretch the meaning of authoritative documents and pronouncements so as to prevent the impression of conflict between them and any experience or opinion that is proven valid but might seem contradictory. To test one's beliefs on the realistic grounds of "reasonableness and sensible humanism" may be extremely difficult if not impossible.[3]

The loyalist is a person deeply rooted in tradition and community, with a strong need for incorporation and belonging. That need is so strong that it cannot be allowed to be threatened by the possibility of separation which too much questioning might pose. The way of resolving the conflict between feminist consciousness and institutional claims is to operate with the prior faith judgment that the tradition and its authoritative representatives are not and never have been oppressive of women, but only appear to be so at times because they are not authentically interpreted. The reward is a continuing place within the life of the faith community; the price paid can sometimes be a burden of guilt, the sacrifice of intellectual honesty, and a certain naivete about the social implications of theology.

Symbolist

Yvonne has been an artist and poet from her earliest years. While other children were playing games together, she would be off by herself, absorbed in the beauty of a garden or the awesome power of a tree. She has always been solitary, introverted, mystical. Her friends tease her about being dreamy, impractical, "spacy." She once drove her car to the supermarket, forgot it was there, walked home, and thought the next time she looked for her car in the garage that it had been stolen! She has often dated but never married, because the incarnation of her ideal husband has yet to appear. She is presently in training to be a psychotherapist, and her innate insight into people and warm, receptive manner give promise that she will be a good one. She is a person of deep faith and prayer. When her consciousness about women in the Church was first raised through reading several good books, she went through a period of anger, which quickly subsided when she discovered, also through reading, the rich though underdeveloped Jewish and Christian traditions of feminine symbolism for God, especially the Holy Spirit. This way of relating to God has now become the mainstay of her faith.

Another way of coping with the reality of being feminist in the institutional Church is to emphasize the symbolic function of the feminine in the tradition and in the religious imagination. This approach also extolls the personal characteristics which are most closely associated with the feminine: intuition, feeling, sympathy, mutual relationship, mythic consciousness. By placing emphasis on the symbolic level of awareness, the person who stands in this position suggests and hopes that the conflicts present at other levels can be overcome.

Important here are the frequent occurrences of feminine imagery in the Bible and in Christian history. The biblical prophets and the medieval women mystics have produced especially rich fields of writing in this regard. Israel as bride and wife of God, the Church as bride of Christ and mother of Christians, Mary as virgin mother and summation of God's creation—all such imagery contributes to the enhancement of the feminine as an integral part of the religious tradition. Feminine imagery for God and Christ is even more significant: God as loving mother, midwife and companion; Christ as mother and feminine Wisdom incarnate; the Holy Spirit as maternal manifestation of the love of God.[4]

These feminine images recur elusively but persistently in our religious tradition. Just as the loyalist finds in her own commitment and loyalty the basis of personal identification with that tradition, so the symbolist finds in these traces of feminine presence a means of identifying with that same tradition. They tell her that the symbolic feminine has been valued and cherished in at least some phases of our history, even if concrete historical women have not. They give eloquent witness to the contributions and essential role of feminine presence in a Church in which the masculine is the consciously operating norm. Thus women can find something of themselves reflected back to them from our faith history, something that says to them, "who and what I am counts for something."

The symbolist is likely to be a highly intuitive person who is able to live her psychic life at a level of considerable abstraction. She is probably very attracted to the ideal of the "eternal feminine" as manifested in the significant feminine symbols of religion and mythology. Key terms are transcendence and sublimation. The symbolist seeks to transcend the problems of history and society by investing more energy in the symbolic realm where she can find the greatest depth of meaning.

One of the forms that the symbolist position takes is to assert not the equality but the complete otherness of the feminine vis-à-vis the masculine. The feminine is wholly other and operates by its own principles which are totally different from those of the masculine realm. Therefore by its very nature it cannot enter into questions of equality or egalitarianism. Equality is unthinkable because the two principles cannot be compared. Implicit or explicit in this version is often the innate superiority of the feminine over the masculine, which does not necessarily suggest the superiority of women over men. To a great extent, however, the two sets of gender characteristics are identified with flesh-and-blood women and men. The idea of mutuality and complementarity between women and men in an egalitarian mode is therefore excluded, since the feminine and masculine forces operate by different rules.

The process of transcending the historical dimension necessarily involves some sublimation. Energy which would otherwise be engaged in the concrete, unpleasant situation is withdrawn from that situation and is redirected and reformed at another level. The symbolist tends to relate to the world at a nonrational, subliminal level rather than a conscious one. Just as in a chemical process sublimation means the movement of matter from solid to gaseous form and vice versa without seeming to pass through the liquid stage, so with the symbolist some phase of the process of awareness described in the first chapter is usually bypassed—needless to say, one of the more painful phases.

This is not to accuse the symbolist of escapism or cowardice. Like all the other stances described here, hers is one method of coping among many. There are certainly negative connotations attached: I had originally called this position "sublimationist," but encountered many objections from women who felt the title was pejorative. I do not mean for it to be. World, church, and families are in need of the kind of symbolic imagination which is represented here. Moreover, it can often function helpfully as a kind of intuitive engergizer for those who normally operate by more rational methods.

Nevertheless there are dangers. One is the possibility of exclusivism and separatism inherent in the tendency to see the feminine as superior. Another is a kind of romanticism which is prone to avoidance of the pain required to work out solutions in actual historical situations. Still another is engagement in the quest for cosmic order and perfection, while perhaps seeking to avoid the disorder and imperfection that are essential to the transformation process. Paradoxically, while most others are struggling with the inevitable uprooting caused by recognition of reality, the symbolist needs to be better rooted in order to remain in contact with that reality. The resulting pain, while different, is no less traumatic. The symbolist must work at keeping her feet firmly planted in reality, even as she inspires the rest of us to dream and to hope.

Revisionist

Valerie is a social historian with a Ph.D. from a highly respected university, and her husband is a successful attorney who has always encouraged her to do whatever she wants to do. She has published extensively in her field and is respected as a scholar. She teaches in a prestigious private religiously-affiliated university where she sometimes team teaches interdepartmentally with colleagues from Religious Studies. Thus she is quite knowledgeable about Church history, and it is from her research in this area that her awareness was raised about women in the Church. From there it spread to realization of the oppressive structures of the present. She is active in women's groups on campus, is the founder of a faculty women's colloquium on feminist issues, and can always be counted on to give a paper or share a bit of her research with colleagues or students when asked. Though university administrators view her with some trepidation, she does not hesitate to speak out when she perceives discrimination. Though quite conscious of the difficulties ahead, she is hopeful for the improving situation of women in the Church of the future, and feels that she can play a vital role in that improvement from her vantage point.

The question posed at the beginning of this chapter is still with us: Is the religious tradition redeemable? Can it be rescued from the patriarchal oppression of women that has characterized it? While the marginalist refrains from giving a definite answer and the symbolist might say that is not even the right question to ask, there is a third alternative position which faces the question head-on and answers in the affirmative.

The revisionist holds that the patriarchal cast of the Judeo-Christian tradition is due more to historical and cultural causes than theological ones. Thus the androcentrism (male-centered perspective) and patriarchal pattern of dominance and submission are serious but not fatal wounds that can be healed. Christianity was born into a world that was already formed into these patterns, and that is why, understandably, it has expressed itself in the same patterns. What is needed then is a retelling, a reinterpretation of the historical data in such a way that our story can be freed from a certain kind of unhelpful cultural baggage which is non-essential to its real message.

The task takes the form of going back into the historical sources—Bible, Talmud, early Christian literature, art and archeology—and learning to "read between the lines," to interpret one against the background of the other. For example, the prohibition on women speaking in church in 1 Corinthians 14:34-35 must be interpreted in the light of the assumption three chapters earlier that women pray and prophesy publicly in the same churches (1 Cor 11:5); the seeming lack of women officeholders in the literary sources of the early Church must be interpreted against the background of the known funerary inscriptions of women deacons and presbyters. By pitting evidence against evidence, the revisionist approach can demonstrate that there is more than one way to read history, and that we have been traditionally locked into only one perspective: the patriarchal one.

The revisionist alternative has produced a large number of books in recent years on the role of women in the New Testament, the world of Jesus, and the ministry of the early Church, so numerous that no examples need be given. This "role of women in . . . " approach is especially valuable for giving women a sense of their own story as women and their place in a faith history otherwise dominated by males who have taken women and their contributions for granted. In a history narrated by men about men for men, the revisionist feminist brings out the nearly hidden minor themes of women's experience. Likewise the literary critic seeing and writing from this perspective is able to highlight the experience of women through analysis of the text as literary articulation of the self-consciousness of the writer and the writer's world.[5]

The revisionist has a sense of history and an appreciation for it. But there is an assumption behind this endeavor that having a different view of history will at least set the stage for, if not bring about, a change in the present. The challenge and the goal is *reform*. Of course this approach rests on a number of rather optimistic presuppositions. One is a quite positive, benevolent view of institutional authority and its good intentions to change for the better once the better is shown, despite the obvious advantage to those in positions of power of keeping things as they are. Another is that knowledge of history will inevitably effect change, that once the truth is known, change will follow. Still another positive presupposition concerns the theology of revelation: that it is a continuing, dynamic reality which impels us forward, whose particular, culturally conditioned past expressions invite rather than determine what can be for the future.

The chief problem with the revisionist alternative lies in the above factors. Were all these optimistic assumptions to be surely true, it would work. But there is no guarantee that once people see that the past was otherwise, they feel impelled to change the present to bring it into coherence. Even if a retelling of history can show us that we are free to change, and even if a careful interpretation of that data from the standpoint of the theology of revelation shows us that patriarchy is neither God-given nor willed by Jesus, all of this is only clearing the way. It still does not provide sufficient motivation for change now. If Jesus did not want patriarchy and the submission of women, what *did* he want and how does that impel us to want the same? That question is more adequately answered by the next alternative.

Liberationist

Joanne has been for nearly thirty years a member of a Catholic religious order whose principal works have traditionally been teaching in parochial schools and running hospitals. As with most congregations of this type, their activities within the last fifteen years have greatly diversified: social work, community organizing, free clinics, and soup kitchens are among the works that now occupy a great number of its members. She was one of the first to welcome the changes in religious life in the late 1960's, to take advantage of new opportunities for education, and to leave her grade school classroom to hit the streets. She was active in the civil rights movement and anti-Vietnam demonstrations. Since then she has continued to be consistent with her convictions by living in poor urban areas and putting her efforts into such things as voter registration and low-income housing referrals. Her feminist consciousness-raising came through her encounters with battered women and prostitutes and the indifference of the law to their oppression. Since she has come to regard the Church as one of the last bastions of male dominance and oppression, she is equally dedicated to strategizing for change in the ecclesiastical structure. She sees herself as a devoted member of the Church whose loyalty demands that she seek ways of bringing greater justice for the oppressed within it as well as in civil society. Her outspoken ways have brought her into conflict with both religious and ecclesiastical superiors, but she truly believes that she is living the Gospel in the way that God is calling her to do, and her sincere courage and conviction are impressive.

Revisionist feminism is patterned on the historical method of analyzing data within its own context, with the expectation of arriving at "objective" conclusions which can then be applied in the present situation. The liberation feminist harbors no illusions of being able to arrive at objective conclusions. Developed from the broader base of liberation theology as it has been employed in favor of the socially and economically oppressed, the liberation perspective openly advocates a stand on behalf of the disenfranchised and disinherited, which its adherents believe to be that of Jesus. It teaches that the reign of God proclaimed in the Gospels has a concrete historical dimension as well as a transcendent heavenly one. That historical dimension can be brought about only by the establishment of a just society which includes, besides the abolition of racism and classism, the end of sexism as well. Only when all persons accept the full equality and dignity of one another can the reign of God promised by Jesus arrive. Laboring to bring it about is the task and mission of all believers who are called to be complementary partners in the service of the Gospel.[6]

Liberationists sometimes speak of a "hermeneutic of suspicion," a critical judgment which begins with the assumption that oppression which is humanly caused must be remedied by human action. That action will not come from the oppressors, but from the oppressed, whose responsibility it is to acquire the critical perspective which will enable them to closely analyze their situation without naiveté.

The goal of the liberationist is the transformation of human society through *conversion*. This conversion must begin with oneself, for it takes a new way of thinking and a new way of being to see life from a different angle. The new angle is the conviction that God's will for humanity, as revealed in the preaching of Jesus, is that we create for one another the environment of maximum freedom and dignity, because only then can we freely choose to sacrifice that freedom for the good of others. For women this means liberation from the world of patriarchal domination in which androcentrism is the norm. It means the ability to claim their own lives and, in the religious context, to claim their own expression of their experience of God and their rightful place in the community of the Church.

Liberation theology does not shrink from taking sides because it proclaims that God does the same: with the poor and the oppressed. Liberation feminism operates by the same principles. In a patriarchal and androcentric religious institution, the oppressed are those who do not share access to status: women. Those women who participate in the structure of power by delegation of male authority figures (notably, vowed members of religious congregations, whose way of life has traditionally been authenticated within the institutional structure of the Church by hierarchical male authority) are in a somewhat compromised position. Those women with little or no derived status (most laywomen, especially the divorced and lesbian who have no male representative in the system) are the truly poor and oppressed of the religious structure. The goal of the liberationist is to enable all persons to claim their own identity and authority without having to do so at the expense of others.

If it sounds inspiring, there are still, as with any position on the spectrum, also problems here. One difficulty is the tendency to consider legitimate only what fits the advocacy position. A good example is the criterion for authentic revelatory matter in Scripture as given by some of the best known contemporary liberation feminist theologians, e.g.: "Biblical revelation and truth are given only in those texts and interpretive models that transcend critically their patriarchal frameworks and allow for a vision of Christian women as historical and theological subjects and actors."[7] Any theory of revelation in Scripture that distinguishes one biblical text as revelatory from another that is not, instead of dealing with the *whole* of Scripture as revelation, is creating as many problems as it seems to be solving.

Another problematic feature of the liberationist position is its close identification with political models and therefore its easy association with particular political causes. While it is certainly true to say in one sense that all of human life in society is political, in another sense it is not. Too close and too constant association with specific and partisan political causes can mean a significant loss of the freedom necessary for critical judgment and imagination. It is probably a mistake to assume that the pragmatic concerns of this generation will be those of the next generation as well. If certain myths and dream worlds must be eliminated in the liberation process, others must take their place if we are not to be people devoid of imagination. Here the value of the symbolist alternative re-emerges as a check on a too-pragmatic analysis of the issues.

Nevertheless, the liberationist alternative is becoming increasingly the one at the forefront of Christian feminist thinking, the approach that at present has the greatest possibilities for providing a consistent method of perspective, analysis, and strategy. It is the one to watch for the immediate future.

This chapter has explored a number of feminist ways of thinking. They have been called "alternatives," "positions," and "ways of coping." Every woman with some kind of feminist consciousness who reads these lines will find resonances with her own experience here and there among the alternatives. Probably few will find themselves to be purely one type to the exclusion of the others. Surely no one of these positions alone can bear the weight of the future. New combinations and patterns of response are continually being formed. Yet I use the name "alternatives" deliberately because I believe that, once having chosen to remain within the traditional faith community and structures of belief, we also have the power and the responsibility to consciously choose our ways of dealing with the consequences. To let them be chosen for us is to fail to assume responsibility for our own destiny.

Chapter Three

CONVERSION AND TRANSFORMATION

In Chapter One we traced the various phases of the experience of coming to feminist awareness, not necessarily with the assumption that one phase automatically succeeds or permanently supersedes the previous one, but that each aspect, once experienced, is important and remains an integral part of the personality of the one who has experienced it. We saw that some of the aspects of the journey to awareness include rejection, curiosity and new insight, anger, acknowledgement of broken symbol systems, impasse, and breakthrough. The last of these was simply mentioned, with full discussion reserved for later.

Chapter Two explored some of the possible ways of coping chosen by awakening feminists who wish at the same time to remain committed church members, and who must therefore live with the tension created by the co-existence of these two world-views. It is my conviction that, while all of these positions are viable, helpful, and even necessary in certain circumstances, they are also "holding patterns," none of which is fully adequate for creatively dealing with the situation, because none is capable in itself of leading to the breakthrough which must come if the reign of God is to be furthered in the Church.

It is now time to pursue the dimensions of the breakthrough experience. Recall that the situation of impasse is one in which all previously known problem-solving methods are no longer effective and there seems to be no rational solution, no acceptable way out. Only a new way of seeing, a change of mind and heart, can make a difference. When the darkness and pain of the impasse experience is fully lived through, not bypassed or shortened, such genuine change can also take place.

Conversion is the discovery of a new perspective from which what was previously acceptable is so no longer, and the desire to change in order to bring one's world into conformity with that new perspective. A moral conversion, the kind most commonly thought of, means change from what is now seen as wrong or sinful, though it may not always have been seen as such, to what is judged to be right and good. The need for conversion does not necessarily imply the need to acknowledge guilt and wrongdoing, however. An intellectual conversion can involve the recognition that ignorance and lack of information prevented anything different being thought or done before. A spiritual conversion can be experienced as a call to a new way of life, with no suggestion that what went before was wrong; it is simply no longer adequate. An actual conversion experience may contain combined elements of any of the three.

What is important here is not what happened in the past but what is recognized as the imperative for present and future. The root of sin is the refusal to be converted and to acknowledge the need for conversion. Sin is self-satisfaction and complacency, or self-pity and despair. The first refuses to see the inadequacy and poverty of the self, whether individual or collective. The second refuses to see that this inadequacy and poverty contains within it the possibility of transcendence. Any genuine breakthrough from impasse presupposes the openness to be converted, which is the ability to move out from self and receive from the other.

Structural Conversion

When the feminist believer contemplates conversion, the most immediate and obvious dimension in which she sees that it is needed is the institutional Church. The systematic subjection, denigration, and oppression of women in the name of the Gospel needs no documentation. While there are certainly exceptions of persons and places, the Christian tradition as a whole, both theoretically and practically, has asserted the fundamental equality of men and women before God and their fundamental inequality before each other.

Sexism and patriarchalism have worked against both women and men in three ways.[1] The first is to dehumanize women institutionally by disqualifying them on the basis of sex from access to the sacred and to leadership. The second way is to attempt theological justification of the oppression of patriarchalism, so that it would seem to be perpetrated in the name of God. The third way that sexism works against all of us is by promoting a "false consciousness" which permits both oppressor and oppressed to blindly accept and internalize their roles.

The dehumanizing of women is the dehumanizing of men as well, for if women are demoted to second-class citizenship, men are allowed the illusion that they alone are first class, that what is done is God's will, and that it therefore cannot be changed. In this way the Church participates in the structural violence of society against women, a structural violence which implicitly condones and even promotes personal violence against them by casting women as victims of male aggression.[2]

Because we are properly speaking here of sin, "social and ecclesial structural sin,"[3] there is a *moral* conversion that is called for. Patriarchalism is a form of classism, the subjection of one social group to another. It is a hierarchical view of human society which makes dominance and submission the operant models of human relationship and renders true mutual presence to one another impossible. Religious patriarchalism further renders a true perception of equality before God just as impossible because social conditioning and the impact of culture are inescapable factors in the formation of religious persons and communities. It puts the ideal of "equal discipleship" (Fiorenza), which is all women are really asking for, beyond reach. It is sin against persons as well as against God.

The institutional Church is called to an *intellectual* conversion as well. Acknowledging sinfulness is not enough unless the perpetrators see *why* what they are doing is wrong. Feminism in the developed countries is often accused of being elitist, superficial, and irrelevant to the *real* problems of poverty, hunger, disease, and political oppression. Similarly, attempts to eliminate discrimination against women in the Church are called selfish and narrow when there is so much to be done by committed Christians in the struggle for world justice.

Those who raise such objections fail to see that there is a fundamental continuum on which all these issues are located. It is the continuum of respect for the full dignity of the human person, which is violated by institutional discrimination as well as by abrogation of basic human rights. It is merely a question of degree. The objection that we do not have time to devote to women's rights, whether in society or in the Church, because we have too many more important things to do is an evasion of the central question. If what we are about is the recognition of all human rights and dignity, then it cannot be that one segment of that task is sacrificed for the sake of another.

Beyond intellectual conversion there is yet *spiritual* conversion. Are we as Church being called to a deeper living of the way of Christ by the prophetic voices of women? It is not only a human sense of fairness that calls us to justice, but Christ himself. It is not only our experience and ideals of democracy that call us to affirm the full human dignity of every person, but the demands of the Gospel as well. Women today are calling the Church to live what it says in this regard. Their voice has become part of the ongoing revelation of God to us, as the mystery of that revelation unfolds in history.

The unfolding of truth about ourselves and therefore about

God takes time. In a past age Christians did not question the morality of slavery; then came a time when consciousness was raised on that issue. Once the truth was seen, it may still have taken centuries to carry out, but that truth could not be taken back or ignored. The same has been true more recently of colonialism. A similar awakening is still happening today about the question of war. Patriarchalism is one of the more recent examples. As with slavery, colonialism, and war, any but the most blatant, oppressive forms of it were at one time seen not as morally wrong, but rather as necssary measures to maintain order in human society. But our notion of an acceptable price to pay for order is also evolving. There is a kind of order that can exist because all possibly dissenting voices have been silenced; there is another kind of order in which the many voices have been listened to, respected, and therefore willingly cooperate. Religious feminism calls all persons to conversion so that together, side by side and hand in hand in a community of equal discipleship, we might work toward the elimination of all forms of oppression and the liberation of all who are oppressed.

Personal Conversion

Thus far institutional conversion. The reader who has persevered to this point no doubt agrees with everything that has been said above. But now comes the crunch: there is no structural conversion without personal conversion as well. Those who are in power positions in Church structures are called to change their ways of seeing and doing so as to bring themselves and the institutions they control into line with the imperatives of the Gospel. What of the disenfranchised, those who by the very nature of the oppressive structure are denied access to these positions? This is a more sensitive area, since those who experience oppression do not like hearing that they too must change. But I believe that the call to conversion is addressed to all, just as the promise of liberation from lack of freedom is held out to all. It is not only the structure that must change, but I too must change.

The *moral* conversion required of women means the acknowledgement of and turning away from the sinfulness that has long been a general characteristic of women: the sin of passivity, of acquiescence in oppression.[4] There are many reasons for such compliance, not all of them entirely blamable on the sexist, patriarchal structure: fear of violence, fear of failure, refusal to take responsibility for oneself, relish of the convenience of being taken care of, selfishness and lack of concern for poor women who suffer most from the oppressive system, lack of self-confidence and self-respect, and, worst of all, self-hatred and mistrust of other women as incompetents or competitors for the privilege of male attention. This is not an exhaustive list, but probably covers all the basics.

As a result of the way women have let themselves be socialized in our culture, their fundamental tendency to sin is to doubt their own power and want to turn it over to someone else (usually male) to manage. It will not do to simply blame the sexist, androcentric establishment for the oppression of women. Conversion requires the intention and effort to cast off the sinful habits of self-doubt and self-hatred, so as to take the full responsibility for themselves that will enable women to be equal partners with men in the work of transforming society.

Women in the Church are also called to an *intellectual* conversion. It consists in allowing themselves to see with new eyes, to admit into consciousness a radically changed perspective, loaded though it may be with new difficulties and frightening demands. It asks women to know what they are doing in the conscious assumption of their own power. Power is only frightening when it is not fully recognized and appropriated into consciousness, but instead functions as an unconscious force which is wholly or partly denied because it is too threatening and would bring with it unwelcome responsibility.

In a recent book, Carter Heyward calls upon women, after
the example of Jesus, to fully assume their "relational power,"
which she understands as "the power to do what we can," in
contrast to established or institutional power that acts only to
preserve the status quo.[5] Relational power is the ability to create,
to forge bonds of friendship, and to empower others. The call to
intellectual conversion is the call to develop clear strategies
which will enable women to empower each other and so work
to achieve their goal of a just and equal society.

There is further a *spiritual* conversion to which women are
called. It is the challenge to live the spirit of the Gospel radically,
from the roots of the tradition that claims its origin in Jesus the
prophet, and from the roots of women's own consciousness of
their uniqueness as persons and their common, universal experience as women.

The claim of the Gospel cuts across all human pride and
selfishness, across all desires that do not have the reign of God
for their center. It challenges women to be converted according
to the image of the crucified one. This has several specific and
difficult applications. The first is the call to forgiveness of those
who have wronged us. The woman who has realized the fact of
sexism in the Church and felt the anger generated by this realization does not feel forgiving, and perhaps does not even want
to forgive, but the one who could ask forgiveness for his exe-
cutioners "because they do not know what they are doing"
(Luke 23:34) asks no less of those who wish to remain faithful
disciples.

The second application flows from the first: it is the refusal
to take vengeance. To the extent that men try in friendship to
enter into the painful experience of women, they leave themselves open to being the scapegoat objects of mostly misdirected
anger and rage. To the extent that they are able to abandon the
defenses of male institutional security, they are also able to be
hurt. Conversion requires that women forego the pleasure of

hurting back for all the hurt they and their foremothers have received. It requires that power not be misused for still more destructive purposes.

The third application of the call to spiritual conversion moves beyond forgiveness and non-retaliation to love. The Gospel injunction to "love your enemies and pray for those who persecute you" (Matthew 5:44) has been a stumbling block through the centuries. It is no less so for feminist disciples. While it is hardly helpful to think of men individually or institutionally as enemies, it remains true that the Church as instrument of sexism and patriarchalism has kept women imprisoned in repressive roles and stereotypes, thus preventing the full realization of their dignity as baptized persons. Moreover, it is also true that certain individual men both in the past and in the present have been personally responsible for maintaining and reinforcing these ideas and circumstances. The woman who has any kind of appropriately angry reaction cannot help but feel at times a "we/they" attitude. The point here is the call to *love* those who oppress and oppose us. Such a call to love does not mean ignoring or discarding the deep sense of indignity felt by women, or pretending that nothing wounding has happened. Rather, it is the call to stretch beyond the anger and pain in desire for the good of even the ones who have attempted to undermine us as persons.

The trouble is that the one who loves is vulnerable, and so the fourth aspect of the call to spiritual conversion is the courage to allow oneself to remain in a position where more pain is possible. If women are to take seriously the exigency of creating a Church of equal disciples, then they must model discipleship, regardless of how well men are doing it. No scorecards can be kept because this is not a competition. Women, who have traditionally been seen as weak, must show that strength does not lie in abusive force or stereotyping arrogance, but in calmly claiming one's own authority and in acknowledging one's limitations and weakness without fear. There is no weakness more destructive than the inability to admit weakness. Those who have the strength to be weak can be effective disciples. This theme will be pursued in greater depth in the next chapter.

Transformation—Effect of Conversion

Any authentic conversion leads from impasse by means of breakthrough into a changed perspective, a significantly new way of seeing one's reality. The change that it brings about is not disconnected from the past, but continuous; it builds on the strengths and purifies the weaknesses of what has been, weaving the old threads into a new fabric in such a way that, together with the new elements, they form a fresh and original pattern. The evolution of one form or way of being into another, the organic process by which persons or institutions become other than they have been, can be spoken of as transformation. This power, present in the growth cycle of all living beings, is particularly mysterious in the ways in which it can be observed in the human spirit under the action of divine grace.

In a well-known and scientifically controversial study many years ago, the Jungian historian of religions Erich Neumann suggested that there are two fundamental aspects of the feminine principle as it manifests itself consistently and archetypally in the patterns of religious expression in a variety of cultures.[6] The distinction he makes holds valuable information for understanding how feminine power is at work in Church and society today, and why its more creative forms meet with the kinds of resistance that they do.

The first and more familiar aspect of the feminine according to Neumann is its "elementary" character which "tends to hold fast to everything that springs from it and to surround it like an eternal substance."[7] In its creative, positive side, it is the mother goddess, the fertility figure of nature religions from whom comes all life, and without whose continual cooperation life cannot be sustained: Isis and Demeter, the good wife and mother whose devotedness and constancy assure the cycle of summer and winter, sowing and reaping, birth and death. It is symbolized by such objects as the vessel that carries life-giving water, and the central support pillar of a house.[8] The elementary feminine is at its best the comforting, nurturing, assuring maternal power that gives and protects life.

In Christian consciousness, the elementary feminine is Mother Church, prefigured by the ark which saved the just ones by carrying them above the flood, who gives birth to her children in baptism, feeds them with the Eucharist, and defends them against the evil of error by her authoritative teaching. It is also Mother Mary, the perfect mother held up as ideal to all Christian mothers. In contemporary Western imagery, the elementary feminine is "motherhood and apple pie," the security of the well-tended hearth, flowers and candy on Mother's Day, the efficient homemaker of TV commercials who is always patient and loving, well-dressed and beautiful, yet keeps a sparkling house and gets a hot, nourishing meal on the table just on time with apparently no effort.

If the elementary feminine has a creative, positive, light aspect, it also has a destructive, negative, dark side. Here, "everything born of it belongs to it and remains subject to it; and even if the individual becomes independent, (it) relativizes this independence into a nonessential variant of her own perpetual being."[9] Under this aspect, it is the devouring goddess who demands blood sacrifice for appeasement of her wrath, wreaks the havoc of natural disasters which destroy crops, herds, and life itself: Hecate and Medusa whose power frightens and brings its victims to the brink of the underworld.

In Christian symbolism the destructive side of the elementary feminine is the witch who uses power diabolically, seeking to destroy the reign of God. It is also the dominating force of the

Church as institution which is capable of smothering scientific, intellectual, and prophetic dissent under the weight of its authority and coercive power: it is Inquisition, witch hunt, and heresy trial, power abused and bent on the destruction of that which will not yield to it. Like the Hindu goddess Kali who presides over both creation and destruction, the institutional Church both gives life through its spiritual resources and destroys life by crushing the fragile spirit of those who resist its unchecked power. In contemporary terms, the negative elementary feminine is the controlling, dominating, overbearing mother figure who never allows her children to become adults, but who continues to live out her own life through them, thus reducing their personhood to an extension of hers.

The Transforming Feminine

The elementary feminine is the more familiar symbolism, perhaps because it is more evident, but certainly also because it is more reassuring and less challenging. The transformative character of the feminine according to Neumann is quite different. Pregnancy and birth are natural expressions of transformative force in that they bring about change and newness, and demand new adjustments to reality. Symbolically the act of baking bread or cooking expresses the same transformative function. While providing food for one's family is an elementary characteristic, the process of preparing it is transforming.

The transformative function moves out well beyond the hearth, however, and that is precisely its power and the usefulness of the concept. According to Neumann, it "drives toward development; that is to say, it brings movement and unrest."[10] It is inspiration and wisdom, the insight that prompted ancient cultures to portray virtues and abstract qualities as feminine. In ancient symbolism it is the Egyptian goddess Nut whose body is the firmament, who swallows the sun at night and gives birth to it in the morning; Athena the warrior goddess and Artemis the huntress; Sophia, the heavenly consort of kings, the creative and inspiring force that resides with the finest leaders; the female Philosophia of medieval art. In biblical literature it is personified Wisdom who is befriended by the wise, who teaches them and dwells with those in whom she takes delight (Proverbs 9; Wisdom 6:12—10:21; Luke 7:35), and who plays an integral role in the creative, transforming work of God (Proverbs 8; Sirach 24).

In Christian imagination the transforming feminine is the religious foundress and the woman missionary who carry out the work of God in spite of incredible hardships and opposition; the woman martyr who "overcomes the weakness of her sex" and triumphs over the power of evil against impossible odds; Joan of Arc, Catherine of Siena, and Teresa of Avila. In contemporary images the transforming feminine is Miss America and Virginia Slims; woman as artist, teacher, scholar, and agent of social change; the successful athletic or career woman of advertising; the feminist as advocate of changed and expanded social roles and social relationships.

The transforming feminine likewise has its negative side: change for the worse, creativity gone seductive and mad. It is the evil feminine figures of the Odyssey: Circe, who transforms men not into angels but swine; Scylla and Charybdis who lure sailors to their death with their sweet, enchanting music; the Maenads who in their ecstatic orgies wander through the forest in bands, drunk with the wine of Dionysus, feasting on the raw flesh of animals which they tear apart with their bare hands; woman as irrational, passionate, and an obstacle to the pursuit of spirit and truth. In Christian imagination it is Jezebel and the whore of Babylon, leading believers astray by the enchantment of false prophecy, false teaching, and the lure of pleasure (Revelation 2:20; 17:3-6).

The contemporary image of the negative transforming feminine is the seductive temptress of TV auto and cosmetic com-

mercials; the stereotype of the prostitute as lure to cheap
pleasure and false security; the stereotyped feminist as irrespon-
sible seeker of independence and destroyer of home and family
values.

Neumann concludes that the archetypal feminine cannot
simply be identified with maternal and earthly functions "as the
later patriarchal world and its religions and philosophies would
have it." In the religious imagination the feminine not only unites
earthly elements, but also the firmament, time and space. It has
to do not only with reproduction and nourishment but with
spirit and vision as well. These symbols reside not only in ancient
religion, however, nor in timeless archetypes, but also "in the
living reality of the modern woman, in her dreams and vision,
compulsions and fantasies, projections and relationships, fixa-
tions and transformations."[11]

Transformation of the Church

Both characteristics of the feminine have their power, both
their danger. Like society at large, the Church welcomes the elementary feminine for its secure, reassuring power. Official Catholic Church teaching in the last century has repeatedly stressed
motherhood as woman's "true role" and "true vocation." In
spite of great advances in openness to the professional participation of women in society, more recent documents still base the
role of women on their "special nature" as opposed to that of
men, which when explained inevitably implies motherhood in a
way that isolates it from the complementary fathering role of
men.[12]

The Church has been considerably less enthusiastic about
the transforming than the elementary character of the feminine
except when it has been safely directed at situations which the
ecclesiastical institution itself seeks to transform. In the work of
evangelism, for instance, the initiative and leadership of women

is admired, but when these same women direct their energies toward the internal need for structural change, the admiration cools. The many ways in which representatives of institutional religion have attempted to squelch religious foundresses, women reformers, and visionary leaders by reinforcing "the proper role of women" need not be recounted. "The elementary feminine nourishes, makes secure, and asks only for loyalty. The transforming feminine demands relationship, risk, and growth."[13]

A major part of the role of the contemporary transforming feminine is the transformation of patriarchy into a discipleship of equals. It is an axiom of social change that those who hold social power will never willingly surrender it unless it is taken from them or they see a greater advantage in letting go of it. In the modern world much of the power of Western patriarchal religious institutions is being taken from them by the sheer force of social change: loss of the credibility of traditional forms of authority, weakening of the power of traditional myth and ritual to convey religious meaning, the awakening of the submissive to their right and responsibility to ask their own questions and find their own answers.

This robbing and stripping process which is happening because of the inability of ponderous institutions and their managers to bend gracefully in the winds of change has its own backlash effect: fear, defensiveness, reinforced affirmation of the status quo, leading to greater rigidity and making the confrontation still more acute. Thus a vicious circle is established, perhaps smaller of circumference with each turn, but vicious nevertheless in the toll it takes in psychic and spiritual energy on all sides. This is what happens in the inevitable situations in which power is torn or, worse, seeps from the hands of those not ready to surrender it.

It does not all have to be that way, however. The positive transforming character of the feminine can direct its energies toward the creation of an environment in which power can gradually and willingly be shared with those who have not previously had it. I do not say that the prospects for sudden conversion at the wider collective levels (national, international) look hopeful, and yet if what has taken place in the last twenty-five years in historical perspective is any measure, perhaps there is more reason to be hopeful than we suspect.

I am a firm believer that forced structural alteration does not of itself produce lasting change, precisely because it does not convince those who hold power that the new way is better. School busing does not produce lasting racial harmony; Affirmative Action does not produce permanent patterns of fair hiring; wage-discrimination lawsuits do not produce long-term fair employment practices; administrative decisions to ordain women do not produce a Church membership that is non-sexist. As urgent and necessary as all these actions may be to bring about immediate alleviation of intolerable situations, they are but temporary solutions unless there is conviction on the part of those with the authority and power to implement them that these policies will indeed in the long run benefit all concerned. Thus conversion is required before true transformation can take place.

As we have seen, conversion is not only a turning-from; to be complete, it must also be a turning-to. No one but a saint willingly abandons a previous position unless there is another alternative that seems more attractive yet equally secure. In the case of sincere religious believers this must also include the conviction that the new position is even more authentic and faithful to the tradition than the old one.

In the call for structural conversion earlier in this chapter we saw that the evils of slavery, colonialism, war, and patriarchy among others have been ways of coping with the need for *order* in human society. They have been seen as necessary means in order to maintain such values as a stable local and world economy, peace, and familial harmony. To this end they have been sanctioned by the Church as well as by civil power. They have

been means, not ends, for creating and maintaining a society in
which those persons whose self-interests were equated with the
common good could prosper and benevolently govern, for their
own good, of course, the rest who were judged incapable of gov-
erning themselves.

In the ancient world in which the Christian tradition was
born and nourished, the prevailing view was that order could
only be achieved by hierarchy, a carefully constructed system of
subordination and precedence whereby the most enlightened
and capable exercise the rule over those beneath them. Those
groups which were structured along more egalitarian lines were
considered radical and marginal. The ones like early Christianity
which adapted into expected hierarchical and patriarchal systems survived because they eventually became part of the system
itself; those which did not, did not survive. Today it is becoming
increasingly difficult to accept that order cannot be had without
fixed structural patterns of superiority and inferiority, of dominance and submission.

This is not to say that leadership and authority must never
be exercised; anyone who has experienced a group effort in
which no one will assume leadership knows that little is usually
accomplished that way. The function of authority, or explicitly
conferred leadership power, is also necessary at times to coor-
dinate and resolve conflict when no cooperative resolution is
possible. The difficulty is rather with fixed institutional forms
which unquestioningly subordinate the thoughts, desires, and
actions of some to the judgment and jurisdiction of others by the
very fact of their position in the structure as constituted by birth,
family, class, income, education, race, or sex. Liberation feminism in particular, in keeping with its origins in liberation theology, calls into question all such constituted structures of
dominance.

A major task of critical feminism is to explore and redefine
notions of order to bring them into line with contemporary in-

sights about the dignity and autonomy of the human person, the need for self-determination, and the greater stability of decisions reached with common consent through dialogue and discernment. With the assumption of full responsibility and freedom on the part of all, patriarchy could be transformed into mutuality. This will only happen if those in power can be shown that there is a better way which is in effect just as faithful, if not more so, to the spirit and intentions of Jesus.

There is a theological tension at work here between post-lapsarian and eschatological thinking. To what extent must we continue to think and behave as if with "fallen nature," keeping the restraints of human sinfulness and weakness as fixed points on the horizon by which to steer a course? This after all has been the biblical justification for the subordination of women to patriarchal control (e.g. Genesis 3:16). But the mainline churches have become increasingly uncomfortable with these original arguments for patriarchy, whatever their attempts to be consistent by changing practices.

The proclamation of the Gospel is that those who are in Christ are a new creation (2 Corinthians 5:17) who can know the truth that will make them free (John 8:32). As Christians we live in a mysterious transitional state of awareness. The first Christians too were aware of this ambiguity, for the same authors who envisioned rebirth in the coming transformation to be brought about by Christ could also cling to old patterns of social inequality and even attempt to justify them christologically (compare 1 Peter 1:3-12 with 2:18—3:7). Recent history provides no reason for optimism that the tendencies or effects of human sinfulness are not still with us: they most definitely are. We cannot forget the limitations, weakness, evil, and destructiveness that they bring, nor can we act as if they were not very much part of our lives.

On the other hand, our faith tells us that something wholly

new has been set in motion with the resurrection of Jesus: we are also given the possibility of being transformed into his image and of participating in his process of bringing in the reign of God, made present in us. This eschatological vision which orients us to God's future renders it an infidelity to use our "fallen nature" as an *excuse* for reinforcing social structures that are now seen as sinful. Otherwise, it is as if what our blemished humanity has constructed in the past as ways of ordering chaos are to be called God's unchanging will so that we do not have to face the demands of God's future as it challenges us now. In the words of Letty Russell:

> Tradition as God's action of handing over Christ into the hands of coming generations and nations is an open-ended process in which the still living and evolving past becomes a memory of the future.[14]

The eschatological tension requires of us that we allow the exigencies of the future as well as the encumbrances of the past to play on the present that we shape through our participation in God's continuing act of creation in Christ. The transformation of patriarchy into a discipleship of equals is part of that creation.

Transformation of Women

Just as there is no structural conversion without personal conversion, so there is no structural transformation without personal transformation. Neumann says that the woman in whom the elementary character dominates relates collectively as matriarch to archetypal images of men in such roles as father and husband, and that this is the prevailing pattern in a "patriarchate," which allows expression only to the elementary feminine. But the woman in whom the transformative character of the fem-

inine is dominant is capable of surpassing the matriarchal role
and expectations; if her transformative aspect is *consciously* experienced, she is "capable of genuine relationship."[15]

Psychologists and historians of religion rightly distinguish
between feminine characteristics and female persons. Some bal-
ance of feminine and masculine characteristics is necessary in
persons of both sexes. Moreover, just as Neumann distinguishes
between elementary and transforming feminine characters, so
some such distinction is probably to be made for the masculine
character. Perhaps the elementary masculine is the force of sheer
"macho" strength, the transforming masculine the power of focused mental discrimination and manual dexterity. More detailed descriptions I leave to others.

Our common human call to transformation in Christ challenges all of us, female and male, to welcome and cherish within
ourselves both sides of both feminine and masculine characters,
the elementary and the transforming. Just as there is today widespread dissatisfaction with the male "macho" image on the part
of both women and men, so there has been rejection of the elementary feminine. Are men who fear women really rejecting the
positive nurturing elementary feminine within themselves as they
project it onto women, and the negative controlling elementary
feminine as they see it threatening to smother them·in the person
of those women in whom it dominates? More to our point here,
are women who fear and reject their own womanhood really rejecting the domineering matriarchal elementary feminine as they
have experienced it in other women and fear it in themselves?
The positive strength of the transforming feminine does not control, coerce, or smother; it entices, invites, and challenges.

As modern women become more comfortable with the
transforming gifts they possess, they also become, in Neumann's
words, more "capable of genuine relationship." This evolution
is today having enormous effects on marriage, family, employment, society, and Church.[16] What is happening is simply that

women are refusing to be only the elementary feminine that patriarchal culture would have them be. They are insisting on their right to be persons "capable of genuine relationship" in a community of equal disciples—no more, no less.

There is a price to be paid for authentic human growth. Part of that price is the conscious, soul-searching honesty required to follow through on insight. It is the difference between suppression and contemplative transcendence of impasse, between going around and going through it. Part of the price too is the need to become comfortable with both elementary and transforming aspects of one's personality, to know and respect the darkness and to love the light. Only the person who has found her freedom in self-knowledge and acceptance of love can contribute to the transformation of a society into one rooted in love. This is the potential effect of feminism on society.

Another part of the price to be paid is a certain maladjustment with time: an eschatological restlessness with the status quo because of a vision and hope of what life and relationship could be like.

> *Future shock* is maladjustment with the present because of the longed-for past . . . *advent shock* (is) maladjustment with the present because of the longed-for future.[17]

How that price takes shape for the Christian feminist is the subject of the next chapter.

Chapter Four

THE PRICE TO BE PAID

In the last chapter we have seen that true transformation does not happen without conversion, and conversion is costly. The cost will be experienced both in terms of the familiar past that has to be given up, and the desired future that is not yet to be attained. The person in this position is caught in the tension between the two, suspended in the present painful reality. Christianity has a language and a theology, based on an historical event, by which to speak of this kind of suffering: it is the cross.

I realize full well the difficulty of using the image of the cross in a feminist context. In the name of the cross "unbelievers" have been slaughtered, "heretics" and "witches" tortured and executed, and dissidents silenced, objects of the projected fear and hatred of the powerful who have identified their own cause with that of God. The cross has been used according to a double standard by oppressors to reinforce their power over the oppressed: the helpless, minorities of all kinds, and the poor. It has served not to help but to hinder the pursuit of freedom and justice. For Simone Weil, Christianity was a religion for slaves because she saw the cross as its overriding symbol and knew the oppression perpetrated by some of its most faithful adherents.[1] The symbol of the cross has been manipulated and abused by the very people who would submit others to it, but not themselves.

Moreover, it has been adequately pointed out by feminist writers that the notion of "bearing one's cross" in passive acceptance has been applied according to the double standard especially to women. Though seen as weaker by nature, women have also paradoxically been seen as capable of bearing greater suffering. The observable greater endurance and tolerance of pain on the part of most women in comparison with most men has been canonized into a conviction about nature and fate, aptly represented by the succinct statement of the twelfth-century theologian Bonaventure: Viri est agere, mulieris est pati (It is for man to act, for woman to suffer [or endure, be passive]).[2] This belief, or, better, excuse, has provided religious justification for reinforcing the passivity of women by encouraging them not to follow the inspirations of grace but to become more fixated in their inculturated tendencies to self-hatred and self-doubt by seeking out suffering, self-abasement, humiliation, and self-denial as signs of God's favor.

Hence it is not easy to speak of a theology of the cross to women who have experienced this kind of oppression and have rejected it as illegitimate and unhealthy. A consistent position taken in this book is that our religious tradition *is* redeemable for women, and that its riches are worth recovering. An important and powerful symbol within that tradition is the cross. To abandon the symbol because it has been misused would be once again to turn over the power of interpretation to those who have misused it. Anger at the abuse is justified, but capitulation to the abusers is not. Rather, the symbol needs to be recovered, reclaimed, and reappropriated into a new context where it will no longer aid the cause of oppression and passivity, but the cause of free response to the claims of the Gospel. The cross can become for women a symbol not of victimization and self-hatred, but of creative suffering, actively embraced, which transforms and redeems.

The Power of the Cross

The cross has a long history of interpretation. Used as in-

strument of punishment by many ancient peoples of the eastern
Mediterranean, including Jews of the Hellenistic period, it was
passed by the Carthaginians to the Romans, and possibly from
them to the Germans and Britons of the North. As a means of
execution, it was usually intended for war criminals and those of
the lower classes guilty of the worst crimes. Ancient historians
report instances in which hundreds and even thousands were
crucified at one time, examples being the defeated army of the
rebel slave Spartacus in 71 B.C. and some of the captured in-
habitants of Jerusalem during the revolt against Rome in 66-70
A.D. Already before and outside of a Christian context, the cross
was a symbol of shame and dread, even used figuratively to connote wretched misfortune. At the same time the image of the person suspended above the earth with outstretched arms was
recognized as a symbol of openness to the transcendent, more
easily of course when removed imaginatively from the actual hor-
ror.[3]

There has never been any good reason put forth to doubt
that crucifixion under Roman authority was the real historical
means of Jesus' execution, probably for the accusation of sedi-
tion. Precisely because this manner of execution was considered
the worst and the lowliest, it was most difficult to explain. In a
culture that placed a supreme value on personal and public
honor, this was one of the least honorable ways to die. The first
circle of disciples were hard put to give a statisfactory account
of why this Jesus whom they proclaimed as Messiah was executed so shamefully as a public criminal, and how his resurrection which they could substantiate only on the basis of personal
testimony could be reconciled with his dishonorable death
which was a matter of public record. In fact, portrayal of Jesus'
suffering and death in early Christian art is conspicuously absent.
It is not even certain whether the well known late third-century
chi-rho monogram, soon used by Constantine as symbol of
triumph, was seen by contemporaries to contain the symbol of

the cross. The earliest certain portrayal of the crucifixion comes still later.

Preachers, teachers, and theologians had to deal with the problem of the cross from the earliest years, however. Different explanations were given, based on differing perspectives and insights. For Matthew Jesus' death was the consequence of his unswerving devotion to proclaiming the reign of God. For Mark it was the ransom offered by the one who gives his life in sacrifice. For Luke it was the fulfillment of prophecy, the destiny of God's servant. John focused on the transcendent symbol lifted up between heaven and earth to draw all to God through Jesus. Likewise the author of the Letter to the Hebrews saw Jesus as model of suffering but, more important, as pioneer of the exultation that awaits us too as his followers. Every writer, evangelist, and teacher of those first Christian generations had to work out his or her own understanding of the mystery of the crucified Messiah. (The descriptions above are of course oversimplified because of their brevity, but they serve to illustrate the point.)

It is to Paul, however, that we can turn more than to any other Christian writer of the first century for theological insight into the paradox of the cross. Formulating his theology within the first generation—Jesus' own generation, for Paul was his contemporary—Paul antedates any other Christian author whose work has survived. He was thus one of the very first to have to confront the difficult question: How can you say that a publicly condemned and executed convict was raised up by God to be Lord and Christ?

Paul met that challenge in three ways. First, he saw the pattern of Jesus' death and resurrection as an image of transformation. The more lowly and humiliated the way of death, the more surprising the opposite extreme of exaltation and new life. The one who allowed himself to become a slave emptied of all honor is made exalted cosmic Lord (Philippians 2:6-11, a text which Paul probably quoted rather than authored, but which he

surely would not have used had it not appealed to him). The one
who was buried in confusion is raised in glory (Romans 6:9-11;
1 Corinthians 1:20-22, 54-57, etc.).

Second, Paul saw this pattern of the humiliation-exaltation
of Jesus as the revelation of transcendence, of God's wisdom
which so totally surpasses human wisdom as to be incompre-
hensible to those who judge only according to human standards.
The cross is foolishness, nonsense, weakness, stumbling block,
stupidity to those who are not capable or willing to see reality
from God's point of view, but to those who can, it is the wisdom,
strength, and power of God (1 Corinthians 1–2).

Third, the revelation of this transcendent process of transformation calls for a conversion on our part and a participation
in the same mysterious process of dying and rising, of humiliation and exaltation, of wounding and healing. If it has happened
to Jesus, it happens to his disciples as well: death, burial, and
new life (Romans 6:1-11); humiliating weakness in which God's
strength is at work (2 Corinthians 12:1-10); meaning found in
suffering by identification with the suffering of Jesus (Galatians
2:20; 5:24).

What is important to understand very clearly in all this is
that Paul, the most eloquent theologian of the cross in the New
Testament, never went out looking for suffering, never considered it a value in itself, and never enjoyed it. When possible, he
tried to avoid it (e.g. 2 Corinthians 12:8). When he saw that it
served no purpose, he sought to escape it (2 Corinthians 11:32),
after the example of Jesus who prayed that if possible the cup of
suffering might pass from him (Mark 14:36). Paul, like Jesus, re-
joiced and gloried in the cross only when he saw that it was the
inevitable consequence of his commitments and life choices.

The Cross and the Victim

Nevertheless, it has been to women and other oppressed

groups that the message of the cross has been particularly directed. Women have been exhorted to enter into the destiny and vocation that belong to them through their superior capacity for self-sacrifice, self-denial, and suffering that has been thought (usually by males) to belong to their "proper nature." Thus motherhood, homemaking, asceticism, silent prayer, nurturing supportive roles, and communication through modest gentleness and sensitivity have been promoted in Church teaching as those roles and modes of communication which properly belong to women.

Assumption of prominent positions in society, work outside the home, professional training and leadership, and direct assertive behavior have often been seen not as advances toward recognition of the social equality of women with men but as compromising the true dignity of women by taking them out of their own sphere and into the rougher world of men where, presumably, they will lose the superior values of home and hearth of which they are the guardians. Rather, women have been invited to participate in and conform themselves to the suffering of Christ by remaining passive and powerless because it is these qualities that will humanize the children they raise and the men for whom they provide a home.[4] More recent Church documents have softened, but not entirely removed, the aspect of the "special role" and "special nature" of woman, and stressed more strongly the necessity of eliminating all discrimination against women and vestiges of social inequality based on sex. The need for consistency between teaching directed to the marketplace outside and practice by the institutional Church inside in matters of justice, due process, and equality is a challenge whose day is just beginning to dawn.

This persistent portrayal of women as demonstrating heroic but fitting sacrifice by submitting passively and silently to pain and abuse, whether the source is nature, parent, husband, society, or Church, leads directly to the image of the battered woman. She is victim not only of the rage of her abuser but the blindness of a whole society that in the name of the sanctity of home and family will do nothing to rescue her. It creates what Mary Daly calls the scapegoat mentality, whereby women are to imitate the victim Christ while at the same time they are denied any possibility of fully identifying with him.[5] Doomed to be like him in suffering and humiliation, they are equally doomed to be unlike him in power, authority, or exaltation, much less to be able to "image" him in sacramental symbolism.

Examples of this anomaly abound in Church history in the "subjection" theme. The anthropology of the Pauline writings confirms the notion of the derivative and subordinate status of woman based on the Genesis order of creation (1 Corinthians 11:3; 14:34; 1 Timothy 2:11-16). Thomas Aquinas in turn appeals to Scripture to note that because of her state of subjection, woman cannot signify "eminence of status" (*eminentia gradus*).[6] Likewise his contemporary Bonaventure pronounced man superior to woman in dignity of origins, strength to act, and authority to govern.[7] The great women mystics and scholars of the Church, a Hildegarde, Gertrude, Catherine, or Teresa, were able to retain credibility and respectibility in the male-dominated institutional Church of their day only by interspersing their learned teaching and stiff challenges with protests that they were "only poor weak women" who by the very nature of their sex must submit to male ecclesiastical authority and judgment. Given the shrewd assessments of the politics of human relationships often revealed elsewhere in their writings, one suspects that their stance of female self-abasement was a calculated strategy for survival.[8]

There is no point in recalling further the history of oppression that has been perpetrated in the name of the cross of Christ. In the case of women, it has been by now adequately documented, at least in the English-speaking world and in regard to past events. If in some other cultures most of the story remains to be told, and if the case-by-case narrative of what is still happening today remains to be highlighted, those tasks do not fall within the scope of this book. The historical task that is just beginning to be tackled is the positive reconstruction and reclaiming of the hidden history of women that has been until now surpressed in our collective memory, an undertaking exemplified by such recent efforts as Fiorenza's *In Memory of Her*. But neither is this the task of the present book.

Reclaiming the Symbol

In the spring of 1984 the Episcopal Cathedral of St. John the Divine accepted for temporary display behind the main altar during Holy Week a four-foot bronze figure which portrays the crucified Christ in female form. The statue, sculpted by Edwina Sandys and dubbed "Christa" by the dean of the cathedral, brought mixed reactions. Those comfortable with the long mystical tradition of Jesus as nurturing mother, as well as many women searching for a deeper relationship with Christ through their own femininity, were pleased. Others found it "theologically and historically indefensible."[9]

To say that Christ cannot be imaged as woman is to say that woman cannot image Christ—this time not only not as priest, but not even as the crucified. Or can she?

> Blandina was hung on a post and exposed as bait for the wild animals that were let loose on her. She seemed to hang there in the form of a cross, and by her fervent prayer she aroused intense enthusiasm in those who were undergoing their ordeal, for in their torment with their physical eyes they saw in the person of their sister him who was crucified for them. . . . Tiny, weak, and insignificant as she was she would give inspiration to her brothers, for she had put on Christ . . . (Acts of the

Martyrs of Lyons and Vienne 41, 42; late second century A.D.).[10]

In this remarkable account, the first piece of recorded history from the Church in Gaul, the slave woman Blandina becomes the image of the crucified Christ to her companions and
a rallying point to encourage them to perseverance. She shows
forth in her own humanity the death of Christ and facilitates the
grace of that sacrifice to her brothers and sisters, performing the
priestly office of mediation between God and her community.
This woman previously unrecognized as leader, whose Christian
mistress in fact had feared that she would not even persevere under torture, becomes the amazing example of courage, resistance, and triumph over evil.

> The redemption and liberation of all humanity is de-
> pendent upon the ability to perceive not only the hor-
> rors of crucifixion that are inflicted upon the body of
> a man, but the horrors of crucifixion that are inflicted
> upon the body of a woman, as well.[11]

Those who believe that women cannot image Christ would
do well to reflect on the suffering of women in light of the stories
of Blandina and "Christa."
    If one part of the meaning of the cross is the mystery of suf-
fering and humiliation, the other side of the mystery is the firm
Christian faith in what that suffering effects, the vision that Blandina held clearly in view. Such suffering is not purposeless, vain,
and futile, but rather brings about the access to the grace of God
which is redemption. It does this not only for the one who suffers
in any given moment, but for all who will share somehow in that
passion in conformity to the suffering of Christ.
    This is not to say that either Jesus or his deliberately com-
mitted followers suffer as innocent victims of God's wrath, or

that they masochistically choose suffering for its own sake because they mistakenly think that it is good in itself. Still less does
it mean that Jesus' disciples blindly choose suffering simply because they can thus imitate him. Rather, Jesus chose to devote
his life to a vision and the attempt to bring it about: the vision
of the reign of God begun in this life. He believed it was possible
and was willing to give all for it. The suffering he experienced
was not imposed but came as a *consequence* of his choosing "with
a passion" to remain faithful to the vision:

> Because of his unyielding commitment, his 'passion,'
> Jesus put himself on a collision course with certain
> powerful forces in society. From this perspective Jesus'
> death was the outcome of his life; he 'chose' death.[12]

So it is with the disciples of Jesus. There is no room for masochism, self-pity, or discouraging passivity. This is not to deny
the terrible aspect of suffering: the wrenching sense of disorientation, loss, alienation, and helplessness, especially at seeing
the suffering of those who seem not to have chosen or "deserved" what they get, and of those we love. Indeed it is precisely
what is *not* chosen, the particular consequences of our choices
that we have not willed or perhaps even foreseen, and the ways
in which the darkness cuts across the lighted path before our feet
that bestow the gift of the cross. For Simone Weil, the guarantee
of its authenticity is that it is what one cannot choose: "Contradiction experienced to the very depths of the being tears us heart
and soul: it is the cross."[13]

The Price of Knowledge

But this is exactly the point. The cross *is* contradiction as
well as union of opposites; this was already seen centuries ago in
its pre-Christian symbolic use. A choice is made to pursue a vi

sion, to opt for living coherently with a perception of truth and
justice; this much is willed. The contradiction results from the
unexpected, irrational, and sometimes violent reaction of misunderstanding and opposition which such a choice attracts. The
contradiction, and thus the suffering, is not willed or desired. It
is conflict, tension, confusion, upheaval. It tears at us heart and
soul because we wish to have the vision without the cost. The
feminine gift for harmony and peacemaking is violated; the feminine original sin of passivity lurks at the door as a tantalizing
escape. There is no point in trying to philosophically see the conflict as "paradox," as only "seeming contradiction." It is true
contradiction, opposites which cannot be reconciled, but which
must be lived with in all their intolerable conflict and ambiguity—as long as, that is, the vision is still worth living for. There
is always the temptation to abandon the vision in order at least
to have the peace of being left alone. But this choice too would
take its toll in bitterness and disillusionment, and thus is not
really a viable option.

Let us for a moment take a new look at an old story. In the
second and third chapters of Genesis, the man and the woman
are told that they may eat of the fruit of all the trees of the garden
save one. They are promised by the snake that if they do, they
will be like God. Instead, they are rudely disappointed and find
themselves worse off than before. The snake's story was a lie—
or was it? Exegetes and theologians have pondered ever since
how the God of the Bible could have been portrayed as being so
cruel as to forbid the pursuit of one of the deepest and most en-
nobling drives in human nature, toward knowledge and understanding.

The man and the woman got what they went after, but not
what they bargained for: their eyes were opened and they began
to see the contradictions in their predicament. They had wanted
knowledge, but were not prepared for the consequences. They
got knowledge, all right, but not the kind they expected. With

this knowledge, they could no longer remain in the innocence and ignorance of the garden. The cruel contradiction of the cross fell upon them, and, like God, they now had to live with its reality.[14] Once knowledge is awakened, it becomes a flaming sword which precludes the possibility of returning to the ignorance and passivity of the garden, and that is part of the suffering. If only we could return to an earlier innocence without the responsibility for what we now know—but it is impossible to turn back without abandoning the vision, and to do that would be such a denial of our fundamental personal integrity that it would do still worse violence.

So we are caught in a web of cross currents which threaten to entrap and devour us. "The cross is no theological invention but the world's answer, given a thousand times over, to attempts at liberation."[15] There can be no pursuit of a vision, no attempts to change persons, society, or Church without it.

The God Who Suffers with Us

The God of the Scriptures, powerful and transcendent, is yet the God who is ever present among us to support dreams of justice: one can scarcely open the books of the Pentateuch, the prophets, or the Synoptic Gospels without realizing that when there is injustice among the people, God is with those who suffer. The prophets depict God as a good parent who must chastise and admonish when necessary, but who is also distraught at the children's suffering and yearns for their restoration and happiness. They do not hesitate to speak with the claimed authority of God when there is something wrong with community relationships: when the powerful oppress the powerless, when there is a lack of love and attentiveness between one group and another, and when the people have neglected to see the close connection between right-dealing among each other and right-dealing with God.

To say that God is with those who suffer need not imply that God is therefore against those who oppress. The social dialectic does not necessitate a corresponding theological dialectic which would in fact in this situation, I believe, lead only to destructive tendencies in persons and in community. As we have seen in the previous chapter, we are all to some extent responsible for our own roles of oppressor and oppressed, which is to say, for our own sinfulness. Rather, the God of the cross is one who desires not the death of the sinner but conversion and life (Ezekiel 18:23).

The focus here is not on who is to blame, but on what happens to us in the process of suffering. The God who got us into this situation in the first place (or did we get ourselves into it?) is present with us. We do not suffer alone, for the heart of God suffers with us. The suffering of God, or the "pain of God" as one theologian puts it, comes about through the conflict between anger and love: God's anger at human sinfulness is counteracted by the depth of love that is also an integral aspect of the divine relationship with us. The result is forgiveness.[16] The only way in which we can enter into that divine conflict, that suffering love of God, is to experience it within our own lives. The conflict between anger at injustice and an abiding love of the Church that refuses to be killed by anger; the conflict between a vision of justice and the price to be paid in individual lives—our lives, my life—to bring it about, that is how we enter into the suffering of God.

The forgiveness of God is not of a kind that lets go of ideals, expectations, or demands. The call to justice and mercy; the insistence on right relationship with neighbor and with God, each as correlate of the other; the ideal of a just society—these demands remain active within the forgiveness of God for human sinfulness. It is not "forgive and forget," as if nothing wrong had ever happened, but "forgive and go forward," building on the mistakes of the past and the energy generated by reconciliation to create a new future.

The suffering of God has for the Christian, of course, a human face; it is the face of the crucified, of Christus/Christa. Our suffering simply shares in and witnesses to the cross already endured for our sake. If we claim to share in and witness to that suffering, we must also be willing to take on the forgiveness it includes, a forgiveness that does not compromise its ideals and demands. If the cross is the world's answer to attempts at liberation, it is also God's answer to the world's attempts to stifle liberation. Once again, in yet another way, the cross is sign of contradiction.

Reclaiming Self-denial

Anyone raised on the traditional spirituality that has come to us from the Middle Ages knows with minimal reflection the role that the notion of self-denial has played in her or his developing sense of what it is to live and grow in the Christian life. A basically good principle of the spiritual life is nevertheless loaded with problems and has indeed been as often as not misunderstood and misused. Mortification, renunciation, penance, Lenten practices, all evoke a cluster of ideas and feelings that range from marginally healthy to downright unhealthy. They connote doubt, fear, and often hatred of self, not in the true Gospel sense of preference for the other, but of a sometimes morbid concentration on one's own sinfulness and lack of spiritual progress.

It was sometimes as if, in our puritanical zeal, anything that was enjoyable was morally questionable and spiritually harmful, perhaps to be tolerated at some times and places, but certainly to be held in suspicion. At any event, the *enjoyment* of such things was a selfish indulgence from which the truly perfect would be able to purify their hearts. Denial of pleasure and self-assertion was in itself seen as a means to greater union with God who therefore took delight in our lack of delight. At the heart of these notions is a profound mistrust of human nature and the created world as ways of finding God, a mistrust which contradicts the biblical worldview and the consistent mainstream of Christian theology.

One of the problems about the traditional ideal of self-denial is that it has been applied unequally to men and women. Self-denial has been seen as the antidote to human pride, a way of curbing and crushing the rebellious will under the triumphant power of God. But as we have seen in the previous chapter, the "original sin" of women is not pride but passivity: abdication of their responsibility for themselves and allowing others to act upon them and for them.

When the ideal of self-denial is imposed upon women, it does not counteract the root tendency to sin, but reinforces it by convincing them that their ideas, initiatives, and normal desires for gratification and self-esteem were, as they suspected, no good in the first place. Thus a woman's sense of herself as incompetent to achieve or even to know what is good for her is reinforced as well, and increasing feelings of helplessness will manifest themselves as anxiety and emotional or physical illness, since direct expression of anger would be too threatening both to herself and to the significant males on whose acceptance she depends.

From this pattern of dependence on outside authority and approval even women religious in highly structured matriarchal systems have not escaped. Maternalism can be just as inhibitive of personal development as paternalism, and in such situations the overall patriarchal structure of the Church impinges more closely on the personal lives of the members.

The fundamental fallacy of the misuse of self-denial is that pesons, especially women, have been called on to deny what they have not had the opportunity to affirm, to give up what they have never owned: a true sense of self. It is only with the acquisition of a good amount of self-knowledge, that is, with appropriate psychological and emotional maturity, that one is able to freely surrender one's own desires, preferences, and attachments for the sake of others and for the sake of union with God. Such self-denial with anything less than the full awareness and freedom of which one is capable at any given moment is not self-surrender but repression. Women are daily forced into such unfree situations by a combination of forces: the outside pressure of significant persons; the inner pressure of their own interiorization of ideals of the selfless, giving person; their spontaneous generosity and natural tendency to make decisions according to values of relatedness.

We have seen that the cross consists in that aspect of a conflictual situation which is *not* chosen, but which must be nevertheless accepted and embraced in order for true liberation to happen. Self-denial well appropriated is the free and willing surrender of the *sinful* self. If, then, the root of women's sinfulness is passivity and fear of acting, it follows that this is the aspect of their humanity which must be confronted and counteracted for the sake of that liberation which is true union with God. Only when a woman has sufficient psychological maturity to come to terms with her own sinfulness of fear, passivity, and paralysis can she become sufficiently spiritually mature to take on true self-denial.

The cross need not be sought in any artificial way; it will be an intrinsic result of her choice; it is the cost of acting rather than remaining passive. The results will at times do violence to her sense of well-being. Her need for relatedness and connectedness must at times be sacrificed in order to allow independent action. Her need for security and approval must be sacrificed in order to dare new ways of acting that may not win enthusiastic acceptance by those who have something to lose by it. Her need to be cherished and valued must be sacrificed in order that she may come to cherish and value herself and what she stands for. Her need to belong must be sacrificed so that she might make her full contribution to the Church and thus belong to it as a fully responsible member. All this is cross enough.

Self-denial understood in this manner takes the self, the true self rooted in God, and turns it inside out. Self-denial becomes no longer only a means to union with God, but the effect of that union as well. Self-denial becomes self-transcendence: the only loss of self that is true finding:[17]

> Anyone who would come after me must deny oneself,
> take up one's cross, and follow me. For whoever would
> save life will lose it; and whoever loses life for me and
> for the Gospel will save it (Mark 8:34-35).

If we are to take conformity to Christ seriously, then we must be conscious of our imaging and witnessing to Jesus in the entire mystery of redemption. The Philippian hymn suggests the way:

> Have this conviction in you which was in Christ Jesus,
> who, though in the form of God,
> did not consider being like God something to hang onto,
> but emptied himself, taking the form of a slave,
> appearing in the form and shape of human likeness;
> he humbled himself in obedience to the point of death,
> even the death of the cross.
> This is why God exalted him
> and bestowed upon him the name above all names
> (Philippians 2:5-9).

Jesus, who was in the form of God, freely took on the cross even though it meant considerable loss of freedom for himself. The resulting free gift of God was exaltation: Jesus' self-denial became self-transcendence and self-transformation in the mystery of God. If we are to find our salvation in conformity to the emptying and humiliation described in the middle verses, we are also meant to find our fulfillment in the consciousness of our dignity of being in the image of God, as well as in the empowering brought by God's exaltation of those who have been considered of little importance (see Luke 1:52).[18]

Reclaiming the Purpose for Suffering

We have seen that women in their position in the Church can image Christ both in suffering and in transforming love. There is yet another aspect of that imaging which needs to be considered: the one who is in the image of God, yet freely allowed himself to be humiliated and to suffer, and was therefore exalted, is also the one who is not served, but rather serves, and gives his own life as a ransom for others (Mark 10:45). As stated at the beginning of the chapter, this kind of language is full of difficulties in a feminist context. Ideals of selfless service and sacrifice of one's own interests for the sake of others have been used continually by religious writers, preachers, and authorities to oppress women and keep them from legitimate self-fulfillment. The difficulties remain.

But I am speaking now in the light of everything that has been said thus far. The first task of women, as it is of men as well, is to find themselves, to lay hold of their hopes, dreams, and aspirations. Once the self is found, the person holds full responsibility for it. How will it be used, given, spent?

> To be in the image of God without attaining the image of Christ is a suffering-free Christianity—which, however, means at the same time that one leaves suffering to others.[19]

There are only two options: to turn inward in search for one's own continual gratification, and leave the suffering to others; or to turn outward in gift to others, and embrace one's share of suffering. The latter does not mean the squelching of the desires and dreams but rather their transformation; it does not mean returning to destructive oppressive structures but taking action to change them.

Dorothee Soelle describes three phases in the transformation of suffering. The first is mute, passive acceptance, the silent suffering that is still the fate of the majority of women in the world today; this is the suffering of the victim. The second is awareness and articulation of one's suffering, more painful still because it has been brought to consciousness, can no longer be hidden, and will provoke hostile reaction; this is the suffering of courage which dares to speak out. The third is organization for change, which can only happen when change is seen as a value and a possibility.[20] At this point suffering does not cease but becomes different; it is now the suffering of the prophet. The sufferer consciously takes on the cross for the sake of the joy that lies ahead (Hebrews 12:2), considering the vision worth the price.

The role to which women are called today in the Church holds many of the characteristics of the prophetic vocation: to speak and act publicly in the name of God to recall members of the community to their destiny and identity before God; to interpret the signs of the times; to condemn injustice; to keep before the eyes of all the vision of the reign of God in its full purity in the midst of historical compromises. The personal drawbacks of the prophetic vocation are also present, and no one should be surprised or deceived about this. The true prophet does not choose to be prophet, but is chosen by God; she does not choose the message, the ways, the times or the places, but they are chosen for her by God; her effectiveness comes not in the ways she expects, but in the ways she does not expect; reactions of resentment and hostility to her unpopular message are inevitable.

No prophet should expect to be liked and appreciated by everyone. It is enough that she is faithful to her God.

There is no transformation of person or society without suffering, and the suffering which brings about such change is truly redemptive, for it purchases at a great price our freedom and salvation, which cannot be had without it. Redemptive suffering is then the heart, the root, of the mystery of the cross. The paradox, and here we can appropriately speak of paradox as two *apparently* contradictory co-existing truths, is that through pain comes life, through voluntary surrender of some of our freedom comes liberation.

Only the suffering will devote themselves to alleviating suffering.[21] The women of the Church who have experienced the passive suffering of oppression are the only ones who are capable through their active, redemptive suffering of being the instruments of Christ to bring about the transformation and liberation of that sinful aspect of the Church for the sake of all its women and its men as well, for the sake of the Church itself.

The mystery of the cross is, to borrow familiar language from another modern medium, what no successful Christian can afford to leave home without. If women are to take the rightful place in the Church from which they have heretofore been excluded, it means taking their full responsibility for the Church as well. There are men in the Church who misuse their powerful positions for their own gain. They are not the model. There are other men in the Church who sincerely and humbly try to live the challenge of the Gospel. They are not the model either. There is only one model, the one in the image of God who was crucified and exalted. All women, every woman, in the Church must take up the responsibility to help transform the community of Christ according to the shape of the redemptive and triumphant cross.

Conclusion

OF LINES AND CIRCLES

The introduction began with the comment that this is a book I had to write. This is even more true seven months later, now that it is finished. I offer some final clarifications by way of drawing things together.

It may have seemed that I have been implying scales of value or lines of development from good to better to best. In the first chapter, for instance, the process of coming to awareness could be interpreted as a developmental sequence in which one leaves ignorance behind and arrives at the illuminating knowledge of full feminist consciousness. Similarly, the alternate ways of coping described in the second chapter could be seen according to a judgment of relative value (an author, like the wine steward at Cana, usually saves the best till last). Conversion and transformation, explored in the third chapter, are in the eye of the beholder obviously to be preferred to non-conversion and non-transformation. Finally, why spend all those pages developing a theology of the cross if it isn't seen as preferable to something else?

These assumptions are hard to get rid of. Yet anyone who has experienced something of what I have described in these pages knows that it is not so simple. There is a certain step-by-step process of coming to awareness, but it is continually rediscovered and relived as we face new issues and new dimensions of issues. I may think that I have come through the point of impasse into a breakthrough, only to find that, when confronted with an entirely new situation, I need to go through the process all over again. I may have worked out very carefully what are going to be my ways of surviving and being effective in my situation, only to discover that after a few years the old ways do not work anymore, and I must find new ones. I may take a secret pride in being open to life and what it teaches me, always ready to be converted and changed by my experiences, only to discover when confronted with God's hard truth that there are deep dark holes in my being, that I never knew were there, which make me hang on with a bulldog grip to the familiar and the safe and refuse to surrender to the new. Finally, I may think I live by the cross until it hits me with the surprise of the totally unexpected.

In each of these cases, we discover that we are dealing not with lines of development but with cycles of experience which spiral back upon us to let us know, lest we had ever doubted it, that in the full strength of our being we are still beginners, no more and no less than the men with whom we live and work.

Probably only those of a certain age and experience will be able to identify with what I have written. A new generation starts at a different point, taking some things for granted which have been built on the anger and the struggle of those who have gone before. Again, it is not a linear development but a spiral of partially similar and partially different experiences and attitudes passed on from generation to generation.

Throughout the book I have used various pronouns to refer to persons experiencing what is being described: "one," "they," "we," and occasionally the obviously rhetorical "I." But of course in the end it all equals the real "I." I as author must take responsibility for most of what is described above as being not simply something I can objectively describe, but my own experience, just as I hope that the female reader has been able to associate and identify with much of what is said. If not, I have written in vain.

It was already said in the beginning that this book is intended for those women who choose to remain in, and perhaps

even work in, the institutional churches and continue to be part
of church life in spite of the frustrations they regularly encoun-
ter. In conclusion, I offer some practical strategies for not only
surviving but (can one dare hope?) even thriving within a structure otherwise guaranteed to cause premature gray hair.

1. Find the persons or situations which will give you the
kind of support and affirmation that you need. Do not think you
can "grin and bear it" alone. You can't. The frustration will
catch up with you before you realize it and begin to produce bitterness and its own kind of "burnout."

2. Be realistic about how much support anyone is capable
of giving you. Too much idealism about the perfect relationship
or the perfect support group will cause another kind of frustration and bitterness. Life can no more be perfect in the Church
than it can be anywhere else—ever.

3. Be just as realistic about future possibilities, so that
your hopes will not be dashed when the next Women's Ordination Conference does not succeed in convincing the Pope to
ordain women.

4. Learn what threatens you: which kinds of reactions and
which kinds of absurd situations. Recognize the early warning
signs in yourself and develop your own strategy for remaining
calm when someone suggests that you are an angry feminist because you did not like the sermon. It does not help to be labeled
"irrational" by those who do not understand what it is that sets
off the explosion or odd conduct.

5. Develop healthy outlets for anger, whether it be tennis,
weeding the garden, or clipping coupons.

6. Learn how to be direct in conversation without compromising your position. Neither aggressiveness nor deviousness
is handled well by most people.

7. Know yourself: find ways to capitalize on your
strengths and cut your losses on your weaknesses. If you know
you are good at first grade CCD and terrible at public relations,

don't take the job of principal out of a sense of duty because no one else wants it.

8. Be well informed about history. Develop a broad sense of Church so that you know what you are talking about when you speak, cannot be accused of giving misinformation, nor can you be fed misinformation.

9. Take the time and trouble to work out your own personal theology and spirituality, and especially how your own way of feminism forms an integral part. Live by them and be able to articulate them clearly and convincingly.

10. Choose your own strategies and points of escalation. Do not permit them to be chosen for you. Do not be drawn into debate about altar girls if you see a greater advantage in spending your energy on training an equal number of women and men to be lectors.

11. When the going gets rough, do not be surprised at anything in the personality of yourself or those whom you had thought you could count on. Pressure brings out self-defensive reactions in people that you never knew were there.

12. Learn to love without having to have the kind of supportive response you expected in return.

13. Have the strength to be weak. Become sufficiently confident in your own strength, rooted in God, that you are not afraid to let yourself or others see that, like any human being, you too have limits.

Be simply what you are, a woman of the Church. The Church of the present and the future is counting on you.

Notes

I. THE PROCESS OF AWARENESS

1. The substance of the lecture was later published as "Inspired Texts: The Dilemma of the Feminist Believer," *Spirituality Today* 32:2 (June 1980) 138–147.

2. The reader is invited simply to recall one of the earliest: Mary Daly, *The Church and the Second Sex* (Harper and Row, 1968), and one of the most recent: Elisabeth Schüssler Fiorenza, *In Memory of Her: A Feminist Theological Reconstruction of Christian Origins* (Crossroad, 1983).

3. There have been some fine new reassessments, especially under the influence of liberation theology, e.g. Robert J. Karris, O.F.M., "Mary's *Magnificat* and Recent Study," *Review for Religious* 42 (1983) 903–908.

4. Constance Fitzgerald, O.C.D., "Impasse and Dark Night," in *Living with Apocalypse: Spiritual Resources for Social Compassion,* ed. Tilden H. Edwards (Harper and Row, 1984) 93–94. The whole article should be read as a detailed exposition of the experience described here.

5. Fitzgerald, "Impasse and Dark Night," pp. 107–114.

6. Carole A. Rayburn, Samuel M. Natale, and Judy Linzer, "Feminism and Religion: What Price Holding Membership in Both Camps?" *Counseling and Values* 26:3 (1982) 154–164.

7. Fitzgerald, "Impasse and Dark Night," p. 96.

II. WAYS OF COPING

1. The most articulate representative of this position has been Mary Daly, especially in *Beyond God the Father: Toward a Philosophy of Women's Liberation* (Boston: Beacon, 1973) and *Gyn/Ecology: The Metaethics of Radical Feminism* (Boston: Beacon, 1979).

2. Recent representatives of this position are: Letha Scanzoni and Nancy Hardesty, *All We're Meant To Be: A Biblical Approach to Women's Liberation* (Waco, TX: Word Books, 1974); Richard and Joyce Boldrey, *Chauvinist or Feminist? Paul's View of Women* (Grand Rapids: Baker, 1976); Evelyn and

Frank Stagg, *Woman in the World of Jesus* (Philadelphia: Westminster, 1978).

3. The criterion proposed by Rayburn, Natale, and Linzer in "Feminism and Religion: What Price Holding Membership in Both Camps?" p. 163.

4. For studies of feminine imagery for God, see Virginia Ramey Mollenkott, *The Divine Feminine: The Biblical Imagery of God as Female* (New York: Crossroad, 1983); Leonard Swidler, *Biblical Affirmations of Woman* (Philadelphia: Westminster, 1979), Part One. Don't miss the cover of Swidler's book: a fourteenth century church fresco from Bavaria featuring the Trinity as an old man, a woman, and a young man. A good example of the symbolist approach that is well-researched and aesthetically restrained is Joan Chamberlain Engelsman, *The Feminine Dimension of the Divine* (Philadelphia: Westminster, 1979). An excellent scholarly historical study that may be of interest is Caroline Walker Bynum, *Jesus as Mother: Studies in the Spirituality of the High Middle Ages* (Berkeley, CA: University of California, 1982).

5. The outstanding example is Phyllis Trible, *God and the Rhetoric of Sexuality* (Overtures to Biblical Theology 2; Philadelphia: Fortress, 1978), and *Texts of Terror: Literary-Feminist Readings of Biblical Narratives* (Overtures to Biblical Theology 13; Philadelphia: Fortress, 1984).

6. The most representative writers of liberationist feminism are: Rosemary Ruether, *New Woman/New Earth: Sexist Ideologies and Human Liberation* (New York: Seabury, 1975) and *Sexism and God-Talk: Toward a Feminist Theology* (Boston: Beacon, 1983); Elisabeth Schüssler Fiorenza, *In Memory of Her: A Feminist Theological Reconstruction of Christian Origins* (New York: Crossroad, 1983). Also important as a liberation theologian who applies her method to feminism is Letty M. Russell, *Human Liberation in a Feminist Perspective* (Philadelphia: Westminster, 1974).

7. Fiorenza, *In Memory of Her,* p. 30. See the similar statement in Ruether, *Sexism and God-Talk,* p. 19.

III. CONVERSION AND TRANSFORMATION

1. Elisabeth Schüssler Fiorenza, "Sexism and Conversion," *Network* 9:3 (1981), pp. 15–22 [p. 18].

2. See Ginny Soley, "Our Lives Are at Stake," *Sojourners* (November 1984), pp. 13–15. The article examines the relationship between the image and status of women in a society and the degree and kinds of personal violence against women.

3. Fiorenza, "Sexism and Conversion," p. 18.

4. To my knowledge this idea was first articulated by Valerie Saiving Goldstein, "The Human Situation: A Feminine View," *Journal of Religion* 40 (April 1960), pp. 100–112, as a reaction to the theological premise of sin as self-assertion and pride; it was later developed by Judith Plaskow in *Sex, Sin and Grace: Women's Experience and the Theologies of Reinhold Niebuhr and Paul Tillich* (Washington, DC: University Press of America, 1980).

5. Isabel Carter Heyward, *The Redemption of God: A Theology of Mutual Relation* (Lanham, MD: University Press of America, 1982), pp. 45–49.

6. Erich Neumann, *The Great Mother: An Analysis of the Archetype* (Bollingen Series 47; New York: Pantheon, 1955).

7. Neumann, p. 25.

8. Neumann, pp. 282–283.

9. Neumann, p. 25.

10. Neumann, pp. 30–31.

11. Neumann, pp. 225–226, 336. For Emma Jung, the transforming feminine emerges from the woman's *animus* as *logos,* which is why it is more familiar to women and more threatening to men, who prefer the security of the elementary feminine projection of their own *anima* (*Animus and Anima* [Zurich: Spring Publications, 1974]).

12. See for instance Nadine Foley, O.P., "Woman in Vatican Documents, 1960 to the Present," in *Sexism and Church Law,* edited by James Corriden (New York: Paulist, 1977), pp. 82–108.

13. John Welch, *Spiritual Pilgrims: Carl Jung and Teresa of Avila* (New York: Paulist, 1982), p. 188.

14. Letty M. Russell, *Growth in Partnership* (Philadelphia: Westminster, 1981), p. 99.

15. Neumann, *The Great Mother,* p. 36.

16. For challenging reflections on its effects on marriage, see Eileen Zieget Silbermann, *The Savage Sacrament: A Theology of Marriage after American Feminism* (Mystic, CT: Twenty-Third Publications, 1983).

17. Russell, *Growth in Partnership,* pp. 30, 33.

IV. THE PRICE TO BE PAID

1. Dorothee Soelle, *Suffering* (Philadelphia: Fortress, 1975), p. 162.

2. III *Sententiae,* d.12, a.3, q.1; see Emma T. Healy, *Woman According to Saint Bonaventure* (New York: Georgian Press, 1956), p. 14.

3. See the informative and sensitive interpretation of Martin Hengel,

Crucifixion in the Ancient World and the Folly of the Cross (Philadelphia: Fortress, 1977). It is surely no accident that this edition is dedicated to Elisabeth Käsemann, daughter of Ernst Käsemann to whom the original version in a collection of essays was dedicated. She was killed the same year, a victim of political repression in Argentina.

4. A good example is *Casti Connubii* of Pius XII, 75, 77. Cf. N. Foley, "Woman in Vatican Documents." I am also greatly indebted for insights and documentation to Jean A. Majewski, S.S.M., *Without a Self To Deny: Called to Discipleship While We Were Yet Un-Persons,* (MTS Project; Chicago: Catholic Theological Union, 1984).

5. Daly, *Beyond God the Father,* pp. 76–77.

6. *Summa Theologica* Suppl. q.39, a.1. English translation in Haye van der Meer, S.J., *Women Priests in the Catholic Church? A Theological-Historical Investigation* (Philadelphia: Temple University, 1973), p. 106. The statement is part of Thomas' argument why women cannot be ordained to the priesthood.

7. Bonaventure, III *Sententiae,* d.12, a.3, q.1. See Healy, *Woman According to Saint Bonaventure,* p. 13.

8. Compare for example Teresa of Avila's remarks about her limitations and need to submit all she writes to censorship (e.g. *Interior Castle* I.2.6; *Life* 10.8; *Med. on Song of Songs* 1.8) with her comments about the gifts and capability of women (e.g. *Life* 34.12; 40.8; *Way of Perfection* 7.8); and cf. comments by K. Kavanaugh about male attitudes towards women in Teresa's day in *The Collected Works of St. Teresa of Avila,* trans. O. Rodriguez and K. Kavanaugh (Washington, DC: Institute of Carmelite Studies, 1980), vol. II, pp. 22–24.

9. "As sculptor sees female in Christ, some see scandal," *Chicago Tribune* (April 25, 1984), section 1, p. 10.

10. *Acts of the Christian Martyrs,* trans. Herbert Musurillo (Oxford: Clarendon, 1972), p. 75.

11. Margaret Guider, O.S.F., "A Feminist Revisioning of the Cross and the Crucified" (unpublished paper, Chicago, 1984), p. 5.

12. Donald Senior, CP, *The Passion of Jesus in the Gospel of Mark* (Wilmington, DE: M. Glazier, 1984), pp. 7–8. See also Jon Sobrino, SJ, *Christology at the Crossroads* (Maryknoll, NY: Orbis, 1978), pp. 201–217, especially pp. 208–209; and Heyward, *The Redemption of God: A Theology of Mutual Relation,* pp. 55–56.

13. Simone Weil, *Gravity and Grace* (London: Routledge and Kegan Paul, 1963), pp. 79–80, 89.

14. For another similar interpretation of the Genesis story, see Dorothee Soelle, "God and Her Friends," *Ecumenical Trends* 14:4 (April 1985), pp. 49–51.

15. Soelle, *Suffering*, p. 164.

16. Kazoh Kitamori, *Theology of the Pain of God* (Richmond, VA: John Knox, 1965). See the combination of anger and love in Jeremiah 31:20, Kitamori's biblical starting point.

17. Well developed by Majewski, *Without a Self To Deny* (pp. 24–29), building on insights of John Sanford and David Tracy.

18. For this interpretation of the Philippian hymn I am indebted to Catherine Brousseau, *What Is the Holy? A Christian Feminist Inquiry* (MTS Project; Chicago: Catholic Theological Union, 1982), pp. 67–68.

19. Soelle, *Suffering*, p. 130.

20. Soelle, *Suffering*, pp. 70–73.

21. Soelle, *Suffering*, pp. 2–3.